WE ARE ALL SURVIVORS

WE ARE ALL SURVIVORS

*Verbal, Ritual, and Material
Ways of Narrating
Disaster and Recovery*

Edited by Carl Lindahl,
Michael Dylan Foster, and
Kate Parker Horigan

INDIANA UNIVERSITY PRESS

This book is a publication of

Indiana University Press
Office of Scholarly Publishing
Herman B Wells Library 350
1320 East 10th Street
Bloomington, Indiana 47405 USA

iupress.org

Manufactured in the United States of America

First printing 2022

Cataloging information is available from the Library of Congress.

ISBN 978-0-253-06375-5 (cloth)
ISBN 978-0-253-06376-2 (paperback)
ISBN 978-0-253-06377-9 (e-book)

We Are All Survivors is reprinted with permission from "We Are All
Survivors," special issue, *Fabula: Zeitschrift für Erzählforschung/
Journal of Folktale Studies*, volume 58, issue 1–2 (July 2017), pp. 1–121.

CONTENTS

PREFACE

Michael Dylan Foster

THIS BOOK IS ABOUT DISASTER AND RECOVERY, ABOUT empathy, about the tellable and the untellable, about listening and the limits of listening. Each chapter was written by a folklorist who explores—explicitly or implicitly—the particular skills and attention that folkloristics can offer in the wake of catastrophe. Most of these essays first appeared in a special 2017 double issue of *Fabula: Journal of Folktale Studies* edited by Carl Lindahl and me.[1] In that context, certainly, each article was meaningful when read on its own—perhaps downloaded from a database or perused online—but we suspected that very few people would read them one after another, as overlapping, interacting elements of a broader discussion. So we are grateful to Indiana University Press for allowing us to republish the original articles here along with two additional chapters. We hope that in this format the essays will be in productive, resonant conversation with one another and that the book will be read cover to cover, adopted for classroom use, and shared with colleagues and friends.

In assembling the current volume, Kate Parker Horigan, one of the original contributors, joined us as a coeditor. Lindahl updated his introduction, and several authors amended short afterwords to their chapters. We also added an illustrated essay on Hurricane Maria and a brief conclusion on how folklorists are documenting the COVID-19 pandemic. These two additional chapters reflect another reason we were determined to share this work now in book form: in the five years since the *Fabula* publication, we have been reminded constantly that the subject of disaster is persistently, increasingly, frighteningly relevant to us all.

In his introduction, Lindahl explains the origins of the haunting phrase we use as the book's title: "We are all survivors." It is impossible for these words not to feel all the more poignant right now, as literally every human on the planet copes with the most devastating pandemic in a century. But the very extent of the pandemic also reminds us that each of us, in our separate isolation, experiences it differently. For all its randomness, disaster (and recovery) rarely affects people equally. Often it lays bare the biases and fissures of our communities, highlighting structural and economic inequities, exacerbating existing prejudices of race, gender, religion, and other factors. Although we may all be survivors, our distinct and often incompatible experiences of the "same" disaster drive home the difficulties of sharing our stories, reminding us of the challenges of empathy.

Even before the pandemic, it was already evident that disaster would touch all our lives in powerful yet disproportionate ways. Extreme temperatures, catastrophic storms, droughts, floods, rising sea levels—all these symptoms of the climate crisis punctuate the news cycle, bursting into public attention and just as quickly fading from the spotlight, even as the survivors begin a long struggle. When I first became involved in this book project, I had never done research in disaster-affected areas. But now I live and work in Northern California, and like hurricane season in the Atlantic, the annual wildfires in the western United States threaten to normalize disaster. In the fall of 2018, a fire ravaged the town of Paradise, killing at least eighty-five people. In Davis, where I live, one hundred miles to the south, drifting smoke darkened the skies for weeks. The air was heavy with the odor of burning—we were literally inhaling the remains of forests and homes and people—and a layer of gray ash coated the landscape. Classes at my university were canceled for two weeks. The experience made clear once more the unequal ramifications of disaster: death and devastation in one community was, for those of us only a few hours away, nothing more than several weeks of unpleasant living conditions. But it also made me realize the ubiquity and inevitability of disaster: now every year, my neighbors and I prepare for the likelihood of smoke-filled air and, possibly, fire. We are ready to evacuate our comfortable suburban homes, with emergency bags packed at all times.

The discussions in the chapters that follow reflect only a miniscule sampling of how people experience and narrativize disaster and its aftermath. But our objective in this book is certainly not to be comprehensive or even, for that matter, representative. Rather, we hope that from the particulars in these essays, readers will extract insights and tools, both theoretical and practical. But mostly, by offering folkloric perspectives on a subject that, sadly, is here to stay, we want to inspire discussion, exploration, connections, and new questions.

* * *

The editors would like to thank Walter de Gruyter GmbH for granting us permission to reprint articles from *Fabula*, and Indiana University Press—especially Gary Dunham and Nancy Lightfoot—for working with us to produce this book. Great thanks also to Vinodhini Kumarasamy at Amnet for shepherding us through the production process. For publication assistance, we are grateful to the Research Committee of the English Department of the University of Houston, and the Office of Research and the Dean's Office of the College of Letters and Sciences at the University of California, Davis. We also thank the panelists and audience members of the 2012 American Folklore Society's annual meeting in New Orleans, during which many of these essays started to come together. Finally, we are profoundly indebted to the volume contributors and to all who shared their stories and insights with us and with them.

Note

1. Carl Lindahl and Michael Dylan Foster, eds., *Fabula: Zeitschrift für Erzählforschung / Journal of Folktale Studies* 58, no. 1–2 (July 2017): 1–121.

WE ARE ALL SURVIVORS

1

INTRODUCTION

We Are All Survivors

Carl Lindahl

THIS COLLECTION INTERTWINES AND ADDRESSES THREE SETS OF questions. First, how do disaster survivors employ words, ritual, and the
material world to narrate disaster? Second, in what ways do survivor nar-
rations go beyond simple descriptions of events to diagnose, respond to,
and heal wounds inflicted by disaster? Finally, what is the role of the ethnographer in a disaster-stricken community? Is it to describe, document,
advocate, or respond? What can we do as professionals? What should we do,
and what should we not do?

The essays brought together here grew from Japanese and American
ethnographers' experiences with disaster-stricken communities. Specialists
in disaster narratives have focused overwhelmingly on verbal expressions.
This collection also privileges the spoken word, yet several of the following studies explore ways that survivors enfold gestural, ritual, and material
expressions into their narratives of remembrance, grieving, and healing.

The paths of the contributors have been interweaving since 2004, when
a magnitude 6.8 earthquake struck the hilly region surrounding Ojiya City,
some 260 kilometers north of Tokyo. Folklore professor Yutaka Suga had
been conducting fieldwork in the region for six years.[1] In repeated prolonged
visits to Ojiya in the wake of the quake, he found that his relationship with
the stricken community intensified in ways he had not foreseen. In 2008,
folklorist Yoko Taniguchi began her studies in communities affected by
the same earthquake and only about thirty kilometers distant from Suga's

community. Taniguchi set about to discover how older residents responded to the trauma of the 2004 earthquake.

In 2005, nine time zones across the Pacific Ocean from Japan, Hurricane Katrina struck the American Gulf Coast. Kate Parker Horigan was driven out of her New Orleans home by Katrina, and some 250,000 Katrina evacuees found themselves in folklore professor Carl Lindahl's home city of Houston. The hurricane affected both Horigan's and Lindahl's careers. Horigan was moved to study narratives of trauma and recovery with folklore professor Amy Shuman of Ohio State University, who was then working with asylum seekers from the Rwanda genocide of 1994. Lindahl responded to the influx of Katrina evacuees by cofounding Surviving Katrina and Rita in Houston (SKRH), a project in which Katrina survivors interviewed one another. The main principle of that project was to make survivors the leading agents in their own recovery. The first SKRH training sessions took place in January 2006, just as Shuman's (2006) essay "Entitlement and Empathy in Personal Narrative" appeared; both the project and the article emphasized the importance of survivors' ownership of their own stories.

Five years later, Horigan, Lindahl, Shuman, Suga, and Taniguchi found themselves together in Bloomington, Indiana, for the 2011 annual conference of the American Folklore Society (AFS), where a large delegation of Japanese scholars had joined the Americans to celebrate the establishment of a formal relationship between the leading folklore organizations of their two nations. The Great East Japan Earthquake, tsunami, and nuclear disaster of March 11, 2011, was only six months in the past, and all of the Japanese scholars present were searching for ways to respond to its crushing effects. Suga and Lindahl began plans to present two panels at the 2012 meeting of the American Folklore Society that would ask broad questions in the wake of the tragedy: How should ethnographers respond to disaster? And how should survivors respond? Participants were asked to consider Shuman's essay "Entitlement and Empathy in Personal Narrative" as a point of departure for their presentations: this article views empathy as a powerful and potentially positive motive for responding to disaster narratives and also as a force that can work against a narrator's power of entitlement, the power to own the narrative and employ it to fulfill personal needs.

The 2012 meeting of the American Folklore Society took place, appropriately, in New Orleans, where Japanese survivors of the 2011 earthquake met with New Orleans survivors of the 2005 hurricane and visited sections of New Orleans where, after seven years, the scars of Hurricane Katrina were still visible. At the panels, two new participants joined the discussion: folklore professor Kōji Katō, a survivor of the Great East Japan Earthquake, spoke about his work to salvage physical artifacts from the tsunami's debris, and folklore professor Michael Dylan Foster, an American specialist in Japanese folklore, joined the panels first as an interpreter who enriched our cross-cultural discussion and ultimately as a contributor to and coeditor of this collection.

Together, we created a symmetry: among the Japanese scholars, there were two ethnographers who had worked closely with disaster survivors and one ethnographer who was himself a disaster survivor; among the Americans, there were also two ethnographers with long experience with disaster survivors as well as one survivor ethnographer. Foster, deeply familiar with both the Japanese and English languages and Japanese and American folklore studies, helped us find a common language and added valuable insights on how rituals and the manipulation of objects wordlessly narrate disaster and recovery.

In the essays that follow, each of us writes of working with disaster survivors and speaks to the role of ethnographers in disaster response. My essay begins immediately below and is followed by a brief introduction of my colleagues' contributions.

All Survivors

By the time that Hurricane Katrina hit New Orleans (August 29, 2005), as many as fifteen thousand of the city's Vietnamese American citizens were en route to or already in Houston, Texas, 350 miles to the west. Very few of them would ever spend a night in the Houston Astrodome or the other giant public shelters that the city had readied for them. Instead, as they caravanned in cars and vans, the evacuating families tuned their radios to Houston's Radio Saigon (KREH, 900 AM) and followed the directions of the Vietnamese-speaking announcers to the massive parking lot of the Hong Kong City Mall on Houston's southwest side (Tran 2005).

Thousands of the Vietnamese fleeing the storm had lived through earlier troubled evacuations. In the years following the fall of Saigon (April 30, 1975), more than one million "boat people" attempted escape by sea, and of these at least 250,000 died—victims of rough waters, overcrowded boats, and the malice of pirates. Many of the survivors who ultimately reached

New Orleans had been interned at least once in refugee camps in Malaysia, only to be detained again in the United States at military bases like Fort Chafee, Arkansas, before making their way to Louisiana. As New Orleans's Vietnamese citizens drove out of the storm and into Houston, many were undergoing their third or fourth life-changing displacement. Jolted over the years from one emergency refuge to another, sometimes helped and sometimes menaced by strangers along the way, the hurricane evacuees knew from long experience that no one else would be likely to help them nearly as well as they could help one another.

What drove these thousands of Vietnamese to forego US government aid and instead camp out in their cars in a shopping mall parking lot? The Radio Saigon broadcasts had alerted listeners that their community—the third-largest Vietnamese population of any American city—would be there to help the evacuees. A Vietnamese welfare organization titled Boat People SOS, first established to serve the war refugees of the 1970s, was waiting with aid. Other Vietnamese organizations and religious congregations (both Buddhist and Catholic) and thousands of Vietnamese Americans converged on the Hong Kong City Mall to shower the newcomers with food, clothes, and offers of shelter. The evacuees showed gratitude to their Vietnamese hosts, but in many cases they seemed less interested in the proffered help than in seeking out their New Orleans neighbors among the thousands of cars choking the mall parking lot.

While the Vietnamese survivors were helping one another, fellow folklorist Pat Jasper and I launched a project, Surviving Katrina and Rita in Houston, that recruited evacuees from the many, diverse Gulf Coast groups displaced in Houston and offered them training and pay to record their fellow survivors' stories. This was the world's first organized effort in which disaster survivors took the lead in documenting their experience of disaster.[2] Nine months after Katrina's landfall, some thirty survivor-interviewers had recorded the accounts of more than two hundred family members, friends, and strangers who shared their Houston exile. Yet none of our interviewers spoke Vietnamese, nor were they in touch with the Vietnamese community of evacuees. As a result, they had not recorded a single interview from a Vietnamese survivor. So in May 2006, I drove to the Hong Kong City Mall to seek out Boat People SOS and other nearby service organizations that might identify Vietnamese survivors interested in recording the narratives, memories, and reflections of those who, like themselves, had been forced to evacuate to Houston.

Representatives of the service organizations told me that nearly half of all the survivors they knew were already back in their ravaged New Orleans neighborhood, Village de l'Est. The Vietnamese community had been among the first to return and had begun to resettle in some of the most badly damaged areas. Much of Village de l'Est had gone under six feet of floodwater. Half of the buildings still standing were seriously damaged, and parts of the area remained uninhabitable. Nevertheless, thousands of Vietnamese were back in Village de l'Est within four months of Katrina's landfall, rebuilding their homes, shops, and community centers.[3]

One of the Houston aid officers told me that his organization had raised $400 for each of one hundred families, but by the time he was ready to distribute the checks, half of the families had already left Houston. "These people move too fast for us to keep up with them. They work too hard for us to help them. They are too busy surviving to take our help, or to work for you."

I saw his point. Our project offered only contract work, with a maximum of $2,250 for each interviewer. Our trainees invested a great deal of time in learning and using skills that would sustain them and their families only briefly.

"But," the aid officer told me, "I know many, many people in Houston's Vietnamese community who love to speak and write in Vietnamese, and they would be honored to record the stories of the New Orleans people who are still here."

"Thank you," I answered, "but in our project, only the survivors can be paid. The only people who interview survivors are other survivors."

The man stared at me in disbelief. "Don't you understand? *We are all survivors.*"

And, of course, he was correct. Although Houston's Vietnamese community had not been rendered homeless by Hurricane Katrina, nearly every member over thirty years of age had known homelessness at least twice, first in fleeing Vietnam and again within one or more temporary shelters en route to their new American homes. No matter how much or how little aid they had received from outsiders, most of them had survived, both physically and emotionally, by helping one another.

The aid officer was telling me, essentially, "It takes a survivor to know a survivor, and the Vietnamese community bond is the key to the recovery of the Vietnamese survivors." He was expanding on what I thought I already knew. He was stating precisely the premise on which Pat Jasper and

I had founded Surviving Katrina and Rita in Houston. We had immediately realized, of course, that many survivors would benefit from the training we offered and that they would all appreciate the money they would receive for recording their fellow survivors. But we also believed that nothing else we had to offer could help them more than the chance to help one another. Many of the survivors had arrived in Houston with little other than their own stories. For them, their memories were effectively their most prized possessions, possessions that grew immeasurably in value when shared with those who would most deeply understand. But the aid officer was urging me to broaden my understanding of *survivor*: the Vietnamese people of Houston had endured so many parallel disasters that they would instantaneously form survivor-to-survivor bonds with the new arrivals.

In the project that Pat and I had pioneered, the ideal survivor-to-survivor narrative was a "kitchen table" story, a shared experience intimate enough to overcome all the forbidding trappings of a formal ethnographic interview. The microphone, the earbuds, the intimidating legalistic forms that the interviewee had to sign before the interviewer was allowed to turn on the recorder—all must be rendered irrelevant. The interviewer would guide the interviewee past these formal barriers and into a state of openness. The interviewer typically told the narrator, "I will ask you a few questions, but nothing I ask will be as important as what you want to say." Our ideal interview, in fact, was not an interview at all but rather an intimate monologue emerging naturally from a bond of total trust formed between two people who had undergone a common loss. Many interviews fully realized this ideal. One survivor-interviewer began a recording session by asking the narrator, "Where were you born?" With no further prompting, the narrator spun out the story of her youth, her marriage, her storm experiences, and her post-Katrina life in Houston. After speaking for more than an hour without interruption and having told her whole story exactly as she wished, she turned to the interviewer and asked, "Weren't you going to ask me some questions?"

It is the shared status of "survivor" that transforms interviewer and interviewee into a bonded pair working to create something significantly greater than an interview; their interchange becomes both a story and a kind of cure. Such cures and stories owe their power to a phenomenon described by Rebecca Solnit (2009) in her book *A Paradise Built in Hell: The Extraordinary Communities That Arise in Disaster*. Time and time again, as disasters unfold, the survivors rush to rescue one another. Humanitarian groups have been aware for some time that "it is firstly through their own efforts . . . that the basic needs of people affected by disaster are met" (Sphere Project 2011, 20–21). One of the outcomes of our project was rich documentation of this underappreciated truth.

As disasters unfold, survivors often find themselves trapped in a pernicious outsider narrative. The legends and rumors that spring up on the outskirts of a disaster-afflicted city tend to cast blame on the victims (Smith 1995). Thus, news reports issuing from flooded New Orleans accused survivors of looting when they were in fact simply finding what they needed to survive. Other rumors accused survivors of shooting at helicopters, effectively trying to kill their rescuers, when in fact they were discharging their guns to alert the rescuers flying overhead that there were people down below in need of rescue. As outsider misperceptions transform survivors into criminals, the survivors become increasingly isolated. As would-be rescuers abandon them, survivors find in themselves one another's best— and, sometimes, only—hope. Although outside narratives demonize them, the survivors become better than they are, far exceeding their expectations of themselves, outperforming the surrounding chaos, and surrendering what remains of their safety to rescue their fellows.

In the end, our survivor-to-survivor documentation project recorded some twenty interviews from Vietnamese and Vietnamese American survivors, sixteen of them in Vietnamese, but none of the interviewers was a hurricane survivor.[4] Rather, they were Vietnamese and Vietnamese American students from the University of Houston. The stories that emerged were powerful and coherent and may have produced healing effects as powerful as those recorded by hurricane survivors. The student interviewers repeatedly reported a sense of bonding with the survivor narrators. Did the narrators feel similarly bonded to the students?

Reviving and Sustaining the Paradise Built in Hell

"We are all survivors." I have never stopped thinking about this sentence and its implications for folklorists. Before Hurricane Katrina, I had never studied disasters and—aside from contributing money to aid organizations—had never acted as a disaster responder. My previous ethnographic experience was rooted in the traditional narratives and festive practices of small, rural communities. When Hurricane Katrina struck, I did not seek out its victims. Rather, they came to me. As some 250,000 survivors poured into Houston, the president of my university sent out a call for faculty members to think of ways in which they could use their professional skills to deal with the humanitarian crisis all around us.

It was immediately clear to me that there were three ways in which a folklorist could help. First, narrative scholars are uniquely qualified to recognize and respond to the false reports that emerge from disaster sites. Although I had not studied disasters, I had studied rumor panics, and the rumors pouring out of New Orleans had a familiar ring. Immediately after Katrina's landfall, newscasters were spreading blame-the-survivor reports: New Orleanians were shooting at helicopters, or wading through the floods with stolen widescreen TVs while their neighbors drowned. Nearly four weeks passed from the first victim-blaming news reports to the first newspaper articles debunking the rumors. The great majority of the crimes attributed to hurricane survivors had never occurred. Meanwhile, in the twenty-six days between the reports and the debunking, dozens of lives had been lost because the New Orleans mayor and his chief of police, believing the rumors, ordered the police to abandon their rescue operations and to search instead for the phantom criminals.

The scapegoating of the poorest and most marginalized disaster survivors is nothing new. Rebecca Solnit has documented the rumor-fed marginalization of minorities not only in the wake of Katrina but also in the aftermaths of the 2001 terrorist attack on New York City and the earthquakes that leveled Mexico City in 1985 and San Francisco in 1906. Carl Smith (1995), in his study of *Urban Disorder and the Shape of Belief*, affirms that the same pattern of stigmatization was at work in the Great Chicago Fire of 1871. The phenomenon is so pervasive and so predictable that I have given it a name: the David Effect.[5]

In future disasters, we folklorists should waste no time in contacting law enforcement agencies, news organizations, and the public at large to prepare them for a spate of victim-blaming stories and to urge them not to accept such reports at face value, not to allow mere rumors to endanger the lives of people who need our help. This is the proper work of folk narrative scholars, and we should pursue it zealously. But such work would be of little help to the 250,000 hurricane survivors who were converging on Houston as I planned an ethnographer's response to a massive disaster.

Second, ethnographers who carefully document the experiences of hurricane survivors can demonstrate that the great majority of survivors are sympathetic characters, deeply deserving all the aid that responders can afford to give. Folklorists were not surprised by the extreme rumors, and most of us tended to doubt at least some of them. After living on the hurricane-vulnerable Gulf Coast of the United States for twenty-five years, I had been around hurricanes long enough to doubt the news reports. I sought a way to hear from the survivors themselves.

On September 5, 2005, one week after Katrina hit New Orleans and two days after the George R. Brown Convention Center opened to take on survivors, I showed up to do something, however small or meaningless, to help. On walking in, I was almost drowned by my fellow Houstonians' collective material generosity: acres of tables piled high with clothes surrounded by hundreds of cartons running over with more clothes. Among these hills of hope, the survivors seemed so small, dwarfed by our gifts.

Their material needs were undeniably great, and they expressed great gratitude for everything offered. Yet in listening to the survivors, I soon learned that they needed something far less tangible and more valuable than their third secondhand shirt. They needed to tell their stories, and we needed to hear them. The tellers were transfigured in the act of speaking, certainly in our perceptions, but also in theirs, as they began to see on our faces that we were finally starting to understand where they were coming from. As a folklorist, I'd been asking for stories for thirty years, but here there was no need to ask. There was one man, one story, that I have never forgotten. He was fifty or so, six foot seven, and bone thin, and he couldn't find a pair of pants long enough in the leg to fit him. As we searched together, he talked far more than he searched, softly, humbly, and unaware of the power of his message.

> There were eight of us, trapped upstairs for four days, old people. Water almost to the top of the steps of our floor, but we were dry. I was the only one young enough, strong enough to feed anybody. Every day I go out the second-story window, swim through that *junk*, get into that empty drugstore—never broke into a store before—pull out some food, but mostly water, cases of water. I twist up some coat hangers and rope, make myself a harness, tie all that water and food to it, and swim back dragging it behind. It took a lot longer to swim back than to swim there. Did that for four days till good people got us out of there. We all got out fine, thank God.

It was easy for me to tell that he was as humbled by his own superhuman acts as I was. Forced to outperform chaos or die, he had been inhabited by a death-denying immanence spurring him to save seven lives besides his own. I had come to the shelter prepared to find people in need, but in their place, I found instead the most remarkable givers I have ever been honored to meet. As the tall man walked away cradling his new clothes, I realized I had not even learned his name. But I knew that I wanted him for my friend and neighbor. I don't know where any of us could ever find a better one.[6]

The nameless stranger told his story as much to himself as to me. It had been less than a week since he'd been trapped by the floodwaters, and less than two days since he'd left the flooded city. I had the sense that he'd told the story just to help himself believe it, to accept that the things he narrated had really happened to him. Other narrators I met while volunteering told their tales in the same quiet way. It was some months later that I learned from other survivors that many people first narrated their stories for precisely the reason I'd guessed, to help them process what they had undergone and to make an incomprehensible experience seem both a little more real and a little more bearable.

Stories like the tall stranger's would need to be shared. These were the true accounts that could counter and ultimately overwhelm the destructive effects of the demonizing legends and rumors. As much as I realized that these stories had to be told, I was instantly aware that I was not the person to tell them. The stories were told by people who had very few possessions other than their own stories; it would constitute the ultimate indignity for them to surrender their stories to me. I wanted every one of my fellow Houstonians to have the chance to hear the same stories that I'd heard from survivors in the shelters, but I didn't want them to hear my version.

In fact, I did not think that when it came time to record the survivors, I should even be the person to whom the stories were told. The narrating survivor would need the ear of another survivor; that would be the natural context for this story. If one survivor recorded another, we outsiders would be able to listen in later on, but we wouldn't get in the way of the unfolding story. We wouldn't break it up with ignorant questions or throw the speaker offtrack when we looked at them with disbelief.

As time passed and my project partners and I found the time to fully transcribe and analyze more than two hundred of the survivor-to-survivor interviews, we discovered a remarkable record of human goodness. Nearly all of the recordings described and acknowledged acts of kindness and courage performed by fellow survivors. Although some narrators referred in general ways to murders, rapes, or looting committed by survivors, very few people had witnessed any criminal activity or even mentioned hearing a specific account of the actions of any survivor criminal. Like the rest of us, the survivors had internalized the false news reports.

When we counted up the acts that the narrators described in their interviews, we discovered that the heroic and generous acts *that were actually witnessed* outnumbered the witnessed negative acts by a factor of more than one hundred to one. One survivor said that Hurricane Katrina, like wartime combat zones, "brought out the best of people and it brought out the worst of people" (Lindahl 2013, 252). But this narrator had not, in fact, witnessed or even conveyed secondhand accounts of any negative acts. During his ninety-minute interview, he spent more than twenty minutes describing and honoring the goodness of the people who had offered him help, but he never mentioned a single instance of survivors committing cruel or criminal acts (Lindahl 2013, 252–53).

Once we began the training sessions, I became aware that the trainees felt exactly the way that we did about the importance of sharing survivor stories with the public at large. We asked all of the trainees why they wanted to record survivor narratives. The most common answer was, "We want people to know who we are." They were tired of being mistaken for criminals, or even victims. They were confident that the narratives they recorded from fellow survivors would demonstrate the true nature of the survivors and establish their goodness for anyone who cared to listen.

Folklorists owe their profession, the public, and especially the stricken communities they study a full accounting of what survivors really do and experience in the midst of disaster. In recent years, journalists and other researchers have taken on the role of advocates in presenting the stories of individual survivors who performed with exceptional heroism or who suffered extraordinary abuse in return for their good deeds. Many of these works have gained extensive readership. Various artful presentations of survivors' lives have been hailed as award-winning literature, from Studs Terkel's 1985 Pulitzer Prize for an oral history of Americans' experiences in World War II to Dave Eggers's 2010 American Book Award for an account of the trials of Hurricane Katrina survivor Abdulrahman Zeitoun to Svetlana Alexievich's 2015 Nobel Prize for a body of oral histories that included survivors' accounts of the Chernobyl nuclear disaster and the Russian-Afghan war.[7]

Yet we must question the degree to which such literary treatments really speak for the survivors or to the truth of the survivors' experience. For example, journalists have discredited Eggers's *Zeitoun* as a largely fictionalized portrayal of the title character (Champion 2012). But beyond the issue of factuality is a deeper question of fairness. Even when authors prove fully faithful to the facts of the survivors' stories, the great majority recast speakers' words into prose more reflective of the author than of the original speaker. And even when editors transcribe survivor-narrators' exact words, they often extract these words from directed interviews or fold them into an overarching narrative that preempts the perspective of each individual speaker. Chris Ying and Lola Vollen drew together interviews from thirteen Katrina survivors to create *Voices from the Storm: The People of New Orleans on Hurricane Katrina and Its Aftermath* (2006). Each story was fragmented to fit into a timeline so that, by turns, each narrator presented a personal account of the first day of the disaster and then each took a turn narrating the second; in the end, the alternating voices blended into a depersonalized chorus. Whose story are the editors telling? By fragmenting and weakening each survivor voice, the editors give too much weight to an impersonal master plot that obscures the individual experiences and reflections of all the narrators.

The best corrective to the slanderous rumors about criminal survivors is the testimony of selfless, humble people who have witnessed and benefited from the heroic generosity of other victims. But folklorists, whose greatest obligation is to "those they study,"[8] need to make sure that the words that go before the public are the words of the survivors and that they are framed and employed in ways that represent the wishes of the survivors above our own.

Third, ethnographers need to be responders. It is not enough for us to learn and to know that legends and newscasts misrepresent survivors in damaging ways. We must make sure that news organizations and would-be responders know the facts as well as we do. It is not enough for ethnographers to learn and to know that survivors have helped one another more than their rescuers have helped them. We need to make sure that the testimony of survivors is shared broadly not only within the survivor community but also among outsiders, especially the media and the new neighbors of displaced survivors, whose reactions have a powerful effect on how survivors are perceived and how well and quickly they will recover. By sharing the knowledge that survivors have been falsely accused, by sharing the gracious and heroic acts that survivors actually have committed, we can greatly enhance their morale as well as the willingness of outsiders to recognize who they are, what they have done, and what their strengths and needs are.

And depending on how well we know the disaster-stricken community, there is more that we can do to make sure that the survivors are given the tools to help themselves. We can help in direct proportion to our power to give them access to greater agency.

These were the three major principles upon which Surviving Katrina and Rita in Houston was founded. But as we went forward, we discovered a fourth principle that came to assume an importance greater than the three others.

The "We Are All Survivors" Principle

In the project's earliest days, we began to discover that the strength of our response was directly proportional to the trust, time, and resources directly invested in the survivor community.

When we first brought trainees together, we opened our session with words that signaled our trust in their knowledge and experience as well as our desire to pass the project's "content control" on to the survivors themselves. As soon as the assembled trainees were seated, we told them, "You, not we, are the world's leading experts in this disaster. We have read about what happened in New Orleans when the hurricane hit, but it happened to you. You know how to talk about this disaster. Most importantly, for this project, you know how to listen to people who went through the storm like you did, and who need to share their knowledge and experience with someone who will understand what they went through." As the trainees listened, their faces relaxed into a look of relief that seemed to say wordlessly, silently, "Finally, we are in a place where we do not have to justify ourselves, a place where we will be listened to and understood."

The first training exercise ensured that every participant would have the chance to speak and the chance to be heard. Each trainee was assigned a partner, to whom to tell their story. Next, the partners traded roles, as listeners became narrators and vice versa. Then, with all of the other trainees listening silently, each trainee retold the story that they had heard from their partner. Finally, the whole group then discussed all of the stories. From the beginning, then, each storyteller was entrusted with the story of another, and each had the experience of listening to their personal story being retold by a relative stranger.

Our keystone method was the survivor-to-survivor interview. As training progressed, each trainee told their own story to a partner survivor, who recorded, logged, and analyzed that story. Each trainee tried to treat their partner's story as if it were their own. With this heightened awareness of the importance of representing all interviewees on their own terms, each interviewer then went into the field to record the stories of other survivors living in Houston. The interviewers took their mission extremely seriously. They were more than employees: they became active agents in healing their interviewees and themselves. Regardless of what the narrators said or what the interviewers asked, the fact that the two met and shared time with each other was healing in itself.

Something else happened to the survivor-interviewers that went to the heart of their healing and deepened their understanding of ethnographic process. In the act of interviewing, each survivor strove to give the narrators the right to represent themselves on their home turf. Because most interviewers possessed intimate knowledge of the New Orleans neighborhoods where their narrators had lived, as well as the street language and social fabric of these neighborhoods, the narrators were free to speak exactly as they would at home, and the interview flowed out unencumbered by calls for the explanations, clarifications, or definitions that an outsider would demand. Nevertheless, after the recording ended, it became each interviewer's task to archive the interview: that is, to write a log describing the content of the interview, to provide transcriptions of key passages, and to explain the local names, terms, and traditions that most outsiders would need help to understand. Thus each interviewer became an ethnographer; each interviewer held a stake in making the narrator's story as understandable as possible to outsiders.

While the ideal recorded interview was as close to a natural narrative as audio-recorded documents tend to come, each ideal log was a work of autoethnography created by the small community constituted by the interviewer and the narrator. Hence, interviewers had to wrestle with the fundamental challenges that face ethnographers. We are all too aware that much that is spoken by intimates in conversation needs at least a small degree of cultural translation to be understood outside the context of that conversation. Although our goal is representing survivors "on their own terms," will such terms carry the same meanings for outsiders as they did in their first, conversational context?

In 2015 a "new" autobiography of the seventeenth-century proto-folklorist John Aubrey (Scurr 2015) was hailed "book of the year" by several British publishers (Malcolm 2016, 37). The editor, Ruth Scurr, had created the biography by stringing together hundreds of fragments of Aubrey's own writings about himself and his experiences. In one sense, the work was indeed written entirely by Aubrey. Yet, as reviewer Stuart Kelly remarked, Scurr's method of piecing together Aubrey's life from tiny, disconnected sentences gave her "absolute control over" him (Kelly 2015). A second reviewer concurred: "If one could find five other people as talented and dedicated to the task as Scurr, one would end up with half a dozen quite different versions of Aubrey" (Malcolm 2016).

Similarly, a half dozen ethnographers working separately to log a hurricane survivor's recorded narrative would produce six different narratives, and it is questionable whether any of us would succeed in honoring the speaker's words as well as would the survivor who recorded them in the first place. Even once the words of the speaker are selected, it is likely that something more will be required to make them clear to outsiders. A certain amount of cultural translation will be necessary. Who is the best translator? As professional ethnographers, we can choose to speak to one another about what we don't know well enough—or to ask someone who knows the speaker in ways that we do not to explain the speaker to all of us outsiders. The Surviving Katrina and Rita in Houston project chose the insider route. The survivor-interviewer became the principal ethnographer and cultural translator.

Beyond the survivor-survivor partnering and interviewing methods, our greatest success lay simply in bringing the survivors together in the same place. It was not only in sharing their stories that survivors healed and thrived. Yes, narrative remained our project's central site of healing, but healing happened in many other, unplanned ways simply as a result of the survivors' coming together. Gathering them in a context that afforded them even the slightest opportunity to work together, share, or help one another inspired almost immediate positive results.

When brought together and left to themselves, survivors solved their own problems, from the simplest to the most complex. Even the simplest solutions could be grand. We had told prospective trainees that the project did not have a food budget but that they would be able to buy food and drink at vending machines near our training station at the University of Houston. On the first day's lunch break, we guided the trainees to the closest campus cafeteria, and they were dismayed by the selection and quality of the food. They decided as one that they must do better and quickly arranged a communal meal for the next day. Each survivor brought something; the quality of the food, as one would expect from New Orleanians, was extraordinary. Each trainee seemed to be competing for the title of greatest cook, but there was no rancor, and the conversation around the table seemed to indicate that everyone was the winner. The meal was large and long, and the length of time the trainees spent eating and talking together cut into the time allotted for the afternoon training. But we discovered that the act of feeding one another and the morale boost provided by time shared at the table more than compensated for the minutes they lost from the official training schedule.

In innumerable ways, the simple act of creating a space for survivor community allowed survivors all the opportunity they needed to strengthen mutual bonds and hasten recovery. We held regular parties. Survivors brought friends and relatives who networked with other survivors to cement budding friendships, begin new friendships, and strategize ways to work and play together. The social strengthening that took place in these contexts led SKRH codirector Pat Jasper to say, "If we could just raise the money to throw a weekly party, the survivor situation would take care of itself."

Thus, Surviving Katrina and Rita in Houston emerged as a fivefold response to disaster. Storytelling was crucial to the first four facets of our work.

1. By sharing their own stories and helping others tell theirs, survivors took part in a group self-healing project. As a result, SKRH received funding from a national organization that recognized it as a behavioral health project.
2. By sharing their stories with their Houston hosts, survivors were able to challenge and in some cases overcome media stereotypes. Through radio programs and live panel presentations, they introduced themselves to Houstonians.
3. By acting not only as fellow survivors but as cultural translators to the world outside, survivors learned how to convey their experiences to a broader audience, and they helped shape an autoethnographic record that offered a closer insider perspective than formally trained outsider ethnographers would have been likely to achieve.
4. Because SKRH was the world's first project in which survivors recorded fellow survivors' disaster experiences, the recordings are special documents. Free from external research agendas, these interviews allow outsiders direct access to survivors' perspectives.

I designed a database to identify the most common problems that the survivors experienced as well as the strategies they used to overcome their hardships. By studying this database, researchers will be able to access an insider's shared views of disaster; from such knowledge, they may learn how to call on the traditional healing strategies of the afflicted community to respond to future disasters.

But the fifth factor had simpler causes and broader effects:

5. Participants soon discovered that they were not merely documenting the formation of new post-Katrina communities but creating new ones. In the process of coming together, members of this diasporic population quickly became mutual friends and supporters. They created a sense of community among themselves that allowed them to adjust to life in a new, strange city more quickly and easily.

At the root of all of these positive effects are two simple factors: agency and community. Survivor-interviewers acquired *agency* and derived their greatest benefits from asking, knowing, and ultimately doing what *they* could do. Many were alive and in Houston only because they and their neighbors had rescued themselves. They had become overnight experts in something far more difficult and important than recording an interview. In connecting with fellow survivors and retrieving their stories, they were eager recruits in a cultural salvage operation, equipping themselves to outperform the chaos of their new experience in exile.

The second factor shoring up the project was *community*. Survivors were so much better at interviewing one another than we folklorists were not simply because they shared local knowledge but because they shared an intensified identification with fellow survivors that fostered an even deeper than usual devotion to community. It has long been noted that people do get nostalgic for what they have experienced in disaster; I have heard such expressions of longing referred to as Schadenfreude or explained by the well-known proverb "misery loves company." Yet when Katrina survivors spoke about the disaster, they expressed the opposite of schadenfreude. What they missed was not the pain, by any means, but rather the sense of becoming closer to their neighbors and loved ones than ever before. They had experienced the "paradise built in hell" (Solnit 2009), the creation of extraordinary bonds that inspire extraordinary actions. It is a redemptive and celebratory state to recognize that you have become better than you were—and it is natural to miss that feeling when normalcy returns, offering craved-for security but nothing close to the heroic goodness that had infused the community that endured the storm.

The SKRH interviewers understood the lessons of agency and community far better than I can describe them, and they all shared the condition of being uprooted from their communities. They knew that every person they interviewed in Houston would be uprooted like themselves. They knew that with each interview in Houston, they could recreate—if only for an hour or so—the intensified community of a paradise built in hell. A displaced survivor listening to another survivor is a combination that can do great good.

In the end, with little money, SRKH directly helped about a thousand survivors simply by finding ways for them to practice agency and strengthen community, while we stayed out of the way as much as possible. Survivors were empowered by the ethnographer's power to be outnumbered.[9] Our power to heal grew in the proportion that we ceded power to survivors.

Who Are All Survivors?

The greatest power for emotional, physical, social, and infrastructural disaster recovery lies in sustaining the "we are all survivors" state, that extraordinary moment achieved in the midst of chaos when participants transcend themselves, overcome self-doubt and personal differences, and help one another in a pervasive spirit of selflessness. Joining the state of "we survivors" is, by definition, not the choice of one person alone; membership must be granted by the survivor community.

Survivor communities are least likely to allow access to those most eager to claim it. The aid official who first told me "We are all survivors" was referring to Houston's entire Vietnamese community, not just the new arrivals left homeless by Katrina. But we must note that most of the survivors whom his organization tried to help had not acted as if his organization were part of *their* community. Without informing the aid official or his organization, and without accepting the money raised by the organization to help them, most of these survivors returned to New Orleans on their own. I think it unlikely that those who returned were aware that Houston's Vietnamese community was raising money for them; I have no doubt that they would have felt gratitude for such a gesture. But the fact remains that at least one Vietnamese service organization and its leaders did not get close enough to one survivor group to establish common cause, let alone community.

It is also true that important divisions and hierarchies may arise within the disaster-stricken "community" itself. Among the huge population of New Orleanians suddenly relocated to Houston, a distinction quickly emerged between "evacuees" and "survivors": an evacuee was a person who had left the city and driven to Houston before the storm hit, and a survivor someone who had been trapped in New Orleans to face the storm. Many survivors had witnessed death or faced death themselves, and they became traumatized in ways that most evacuees did not experience. During the first day of each SKRH training school, all participants listened in turn to each trainee's narrative, and in every group, there was at least one evacuee who pronounced her story unworthy to stand alongside the stories of the survivors. In our second school, evacuee Dione Morgan stated, "I'm in awe of Vincent's story," referring to the narrative of Vincent Trotter, a New Orleans prison guard who spent the three days following Katrina's landfall trapped with hundreds of desperate prisoners on an overpass surrounded by floodwater. As Dione expressed her sense of inadequacy, several of the evacuees seated in the circle of trainees nodded to signify that they shared her feelings. In our role as facilitators, Pat Jasper and I tried to assure all that each participant—whether survivor or evacuee—had a story well worth telling. But our role was secondary: it was the survivors themselves who welcomed the evacuees into their midst and greeted them as equals. I can recall only one instance of an attempt by one participant to disenfranchise another. One evacuee who had spent years in New Orleans faced off with an evacuee who had moved into the city just weeks before the hurricane and told him, "You don't have the experience to do this work." But by far the greater tendency was the opposite: to extend the title of *survivor* to anyone who had suffered in some way from the disaster. And the distance between evacuees and survivors diminished the longer the two groups, forced to conclude that they would likely never be able to return to New Orleans, endured their common exile. There was significant evidence that the survivors as a group were more traumatized than the evacuees; it is also true that the evacuee interviewers recorded and processed far more interviews per capita than did the survivor-interviewers.[10] Yet the survivors strengthened the project in other ways: as panel speakers, as friends, as supporters of all those New Orleanians exiled in Houston. In the course of our project, hundreds of survivors were interviewed by evacuees, and evidence strongly suggests that these survivors would readily embrace their interviewers with the statement "We are all survivors."

With disasters around the world steadily growing in scale and frequency, ethnographers must ask themselves whether it is enough merely to research survivors' narratives or whether, rather, we are charged to do more. How should we respond? Each of the contributors to this collection, like the Katrina evacuees in Houston, has felt the lack of power to do enough. We have all felt awe of the survivors with whom we have worked. And, as professionals, each of us has witnessed or read of ethnographers who, regardless of their intentions, inflicted harm on survivors in the course of conducting research (as Suga's contribution to our collection attests). In 2012, after attending an international conference on "Catastrophe and Constructing Communities" in Osaka, Kōji Katō and I flew to his hometown of Sendai, where he introduced me to survivors of the Great East Japan Earthquake. Among them was Mrs. Mihoko Murakami, a leader of some three hundred tsunami survivors living in temporary housing twenty months after their homes were washed away. "I tell the story of the tsunami so that others will not have to," she said to me. She then spoke of a group of anthropologists who had approached the children in her community and asked them to describe their tsunami experiences. The children, Murakami-san told me, "shouted at the anthropologists, 'Go away! If you want to talk about the tsunami, don't talk to us. Go away!'"

None of the contributors to this collection would have acted as thoughtlessly cruel as the child-accosting anthropologists berated by Murakami-san. But at various times we have all asked ourselves whether we were doing more harm than good. Yoko Taniguchi's essay recalls her feeling of doubt and her reluctance to ask survivors about painful experiences. Each of us may have wondered at times whether we shouldn't go away. What good are we really doing? If we don't go away, where do we go? If we stay, what do we do? What are the best uses of our empathy? What can we do to ensure the entitlement of the survivors with whom we work? The answers posed by the contributors tend to minimize their own claims to membership in any survivor community. Yet I doubt that any of the survivors with whom these colleagues have worked would ever ask them to go away.

Yutaka Suga, professor of folkloristics at the Institute for Advanced Studies on Asia, University of Tokyo, did not go away. He has worked steadily with the disaster-stricken community of Ojiya since the earthquake of 2004. His article makes a case for the constructive power of empathy. Moreover, he narrates his attempts to learn about the community through engagement in its activities, most notably in raising a fighting bull and joining in the distinctive and dangerous tradition of bullfighting revered in the village. His account suggests to me that Ojiya has granted him a level of acceptance that he would not himself claim. Although he certainly would not call himself a survivor, I wonder if the citizens of Ojiya would: in 2016, Suga was hospitalized for weeks for an injury that he sustained in the bullring—an injury that, I believe, would strike Ojiya residents as emblematic of a heart-and-soul commitment to their village.

For thirteen years, Yoko Taniguchi—currently lecturer at Musashino Art University and Meiji Gakuin University—has centered research in Yamakoshi, just thirty kilometers from Suga's field community, Ojiya. Both towns were devastated by a 2004 earthquake, and Yamakoshi was uninhabited for three years before survivors returned. Taniguchi has worked closely with older citizens. She reflects on her developing relationship with community members, their resistance to being seen as victims, and their desire to emphasize the story of their recovery, to speak about how they healed rather than about how they suffered. The essay describes the self-healing gestures and strategies employed by villagers as they recovered from the disaster, returned to their homes, and resumed their daily lives.

Professor Kōji Katō (formerly of Tohoku Gakuin University and now of Musashino Art University) became a tsunami survivor before becoming a disaster scholar. He lost his home and his best friend to the Great East Japan Earthquake of 2011. As he and his family sought and then settled into a new home, Katō's work as a museum curator led him to undertake the salvage work described in his essay. His contribution raises and addresses crucial questions concerning the power of lifeless objects to narrate disaster as well as to inspire verbal narratives that serve to reclaim missing artifacts and repurpose those that remain.

Kate Parker Horigan, whose experience of Hurricane Katrina led her into the field of folklore, is now associate professor of folk studies at Western Kentucky University. Like Kōji Katō, she was a disaster survivor before becoming a disaster scholar. Her meditations on the questions of who narrates, and who should narrate, disaster experiences; her attention to how one narrates such experiences; and her considerations of which survivor speaks or does not speak for another survivor constitute essential reading for our shared enterprise.

It was Amy Shuman, professor of folklore at the Ohio State University, who first formulated the scholarly binary of empathy and entitlement that all of the contributors address to one extent or another. Here, building on her long work with survivors of the Rwandan genocide of 1994, she reviews the complex history of *empathy* as understood and enacted by ethnographers, psychologists, and specialists in trauma and disability studies, among other groups, offering a close consideration of empathy as both "a necessary and insufficient response to trauma," a charge to tell what is essentially untellable.

Michael Dylan Foster, professor of East Asian languages and cultures at the University of California, Davis, has devoted much of his recent research to the concept of intangible cultural heritage (ICH) in general and Japanese New Year's rituals in particular. He presents a meditation on ways in which rituals express and teach community resilience and interdependence in the face of disaster. Foster's essay humbly declares his personal distance from the disaster sites and communities discussed here, but it also bears witness to how much can be learned, how many questions can be opened up, how many explorations can begin, when outsiders combine empathy and modesty.

In the five brief years since this collection was first published, the tenth anniversary of the Great East Japan Earthquake and the fifteenth of Hurricane Katrina have passed, but the relevance of the questions addressed here has only grown, apace with the number, frequency, and intensity of disasters worldwide. Fittingly, our final two chapters present ethnographers' responses to two disasters that postdate our first edition.

Gloria M. Colom Braña was a doctoral student conducting fieldwork in Puerto Rico in September 2017 when Hurricane Maria struck. Maria, the most devastating hurricane of the hyperactive 2017 season, killed an estimated 2,975 Puerto Ricans and so thoroughly disabled the island's infrastructure that six months later nearly half a million people remained without electric power and the entire island continued to suffer periodic blackouts. It was six months after Maria's landfall that Colom Braña pieced together a written account of the storm's approach, landfall, and aftermath, focused particularly on ways in which her family members and neighbors relied on their traditions and ingenuity to endure. Her account fully verifies what on-the-ground responders have long known: that "it is firstly through their own efforts . . . that the basic needs of people affected by disaster are met" (Sphere Project 2011, 20–21). Her illustrations expand her expressive range into places where words alone cannot serve.

In the final offering, Georgia Ellie Dassler joins with coeditor Kate Parker Horigan to chronicle the most inescapable of ongoing disasters, the

COVID-19 pandemic, which began in late 2019 and which has inflicted well over six million fatalities as we go to press. Dassler, who completed her MA in folk studies at Western Kentucky University in 2021, interviewed seven public folklorists who feel a need to respond to the pandemic—and are currently conceptualizing and experimenting with ways of practicing and sharing traditional arts in a context of mutual isolation.

Several of the original contributors have added afterwords presenting their most recent work and insights. For me, the primary takeaway of the past five years has been the deepening conviction that the survivor knows best. The best thing I can do is listen, trust, and furnish access to the tools and communities that survivors seek, for the purposes they judge most important. The SKRH project succeeded as a mental health project largely because most of the survivor-interviewers did not think of it as a mental health project. Rather, they saw themselves doing something useful and valuable with and for others.

All of the responses described and discussed in this book ultimately raise the issue of survivor agency.[11] Such agency is itself an issue of necessity. In massive disasters—like the Japanese earthquakes, the American hurricanes, the Rwandan genocide—survivor agency is not only the best way to respond; it is most often the only effective way. The survivors vastly outnumber the professional responders, and they are passionately willing to give to their fellows in any way they can. They know better than outsiders what they can do and what tools they need to do it. They need to help, and we are just beginning to realize how much we need their help. This is something that ethnographers know as well as anyone. We did not learn it from books or from talking to other academics; we learned it from the communities that have honored us with their prodigious local knowledge. They have lent us this knowledge, and it is time for us to use it in repaying them.[12]

Notes

1. For the sake of clarity, throughout this book the names of Japanese contributors are presented in Western name order with given name preceding family name.

2. The inception and uniqueness of SKRH are described in greater detail than space allows here in Lindahl (2012, 2013), Jasper and Lindahl (2007), and Lindahl et al. (2009).

3. The damage inflicted on Village de l'Est and the post-disaster Vietnamese resettlement of this area are documented in City of New Orleans (n.d.) and Vanlandingham (2015).

4. Between January 2006 and January 2009, the Surviving Katrina and Rita in Houston project deposited 433 interviews in the Houston Folklore Archive, now housed in Special Collections at the University of Houston's M. D. Anderson Library. One hundred five of the

interviews are also on deposit at the American Folklife Center in the Library of Congress, Washington, DC. Many publications, exhibits, and radio broadcasts—including Jasper and Lindahl (2007), Lindahl (2007, 2012, 2013), Lindahl and Nash (2008), Lindahl et al. (2009), and McNamara et al. (2007–9)—draw upon these interviews. Unpublished references to the interviews are drawn from the Surviving Katrina and Rita in Houston database, a work in progress that catalogs the interviews, including more than 200 complete transcriptions and 149 completely keyworded interview records.

5. The term *David Effect* was coined in response to Fine's use of "Goliath Effect" to refer to the tendency of corporate rumors to target the largest and best-known corporations. Rumors of food and drink contamination, for example, are more likely to name the giant manufacturers like McDonald's and Coca-Cola than smaller companies. In the wake of the disaster, however, accusations tend to point in the opposite direction: it is the poorest and least powerful minorities that are blamed for disorder and violence; see Fine (1985) and Lindahl (2012, 148–52).

6. An earlier description of the tall stranger and his narrative appears in Lindahl (2007, 1527).

7. The award-winning disaster oral histories of these authors include Terkel (1984), Eggers (2009), Alexievich (2005), and Alexievich (1992).

8. The phrase that folklorists' first obligation is to "those they study" is quoted from the American Folklore Society's "Statement on Ethics" (1988).

9. For further discussions of "the power to be outnumbered," see Lindahl (1997, 2003).

10. In 2007, psychology doctoral student Jenna Baddeley used techniques pioneered by her mentor, James A. Pennebaker (1995, 1997), in an attempt to discover whether survivors had been more traumatized by Katrina than evacuees had been. She conducted a blind study of categories of words spoken by interviewees (e.g., frequency of *I* as opposed to *we*, and frequency of active as opposed to passive vocabulary); the results were then sorted according to two criteria: the age of the interviewee and the interviewee's status as either an evacuee or a survivor. There were notable differences between adult evacuees and adult survivors, including survivors' greater use of *we* as opposed to *I* and survivors' greater use of active verbs and words indicative of anger; see Lindahl et al. (2009, 71–76).

11. As part of their continuing commitment to enhancing the role of survivor agency in disaster recovery, Professors Horigan, Katō, Lindahl, and Shuman met in Bellagio, Italy, in July 2014 at a conference titled "Survivor-Centered Responses to Massive Disasters" to become cofounders of the International Commission on Survivor-Centered Disaster Recovery.

12. This chapter is dedicated in gratitude to all the Katrina survivors who shared their stories and goodwill with the Surviving Katrina and Rita in Houston project, and to Mrs. Mihoko Murakami and Professor Kōji Katō for sharing the wisdom they derived from enduring and responding to the Great East Japan Earthquake.

References

Alexievich, Svetlana. 1992. *Zinky Boys: Soviet Voices from the Afghanistan War*. Translated by Julia Whitby and Robin Whitby. New York: Norton. Published in Russian, 1990.
———. 2005. *Voices from Chernobyl: The Oral History of a Nuclear Disaster*. Translated by Keith Gessen. Normal, IL: Dalkey Archive. Published in Russian, 1997.

American Folklore Society. 1988. "AFS Statement on Ethics: Principles of Professional Responsibility." *AFS News*, n.s., 17, no. 1 (February). https://americanfolkloresociety .org/our-work/position-statement-ethics/.

Ancelet, Barry J., Marcia Gaudet, and Carl Lindahl. 2013. *Second Line Rescue: Improvised Responses to Katrina and Rita*. Jackson: University Press of Mississippi.

Champion, Edward. 2012. "Dave Eggers, National Book Award Finalist, Refuses to Answer about Abdulrahman Zeitoun's Violent Assaults." *Reluctant Habits*, November 14. http://www.edrants.com/dave-eggers-national-book-award-finalist-refuses-to-answer -about-abdulrahman-zeitouns-violent-assaults/.

City of New Orleans. n.d. *Village de l'Est Neighborhood, Planning District 10*. New Orleans: City of New Orleans. Accessed April 29, 2021. http://nola.gov/getmedia/70c8f7ee -950a-4159-8911-7ed402eb3a39/District_10_Final_Village-de-Lest.pdf/.

Eggers, Dave. 2009. *Zeitoun*. San Francisco: McSweeney's.

Fine, Gary Alan. 1985. "The Goliath Effect: Corporate Dominance and Mercantile Legends." *Journal of American Folklore* 98 (387): 63–84.

Jasper, Pat, and Carl Lindahl. 2007. "The Houston Survivor Project: An Introduction." In "American Tragedy: New Orleans under Water," special issue, *Callaloo* 29 (4): 1504–5.

Kelly, Stuart. 2015. "Enter John Aubrey." *London Times Literary Supplement*, February 25, 2015. http://www.the-tls.co.uk/articles/public/enter-john-aubrey/.

Lindahl, Carl. 1997. "The Power of Being Outnumbered." *Louisiana Folklore Miscellany* 12: 43–76.

———. 2003. "Finding the Field through the Detour of the Self." In *Working the Field: Accounts from French Louisiana*, edited by Jacques Henry and Sara LeMenestral, 3–22. Westport, CT: Praeger.

———, ed. 2007. "Section on the Surviving Katrina and Rita in Houston Project." In "American Tragedy: New Orleans under Water," special issue, *Callaloo* 29 (4): 1504–38.

———. 2012. "Legends of Hurricane Katrina: The Right to Be Wrong, Survivor-to-Survivor Storytelling, and Healing." *Journal of American Folklore* 125 (496): 139–76.

———. 2013. "Vernacular Self-Rescue: 'Victims' Save One Another and Themselves." In *Second Line Rescue: Improvised Responses to Katrina and Rita*, edited by Barry J. Ancelet, Marcia Gaudet, and Carl Lindahl, 91–259. Jackson: University Press of Mississippi.

Lindahl, Carl, Jenna Baddeley, Sue Nash, Shari Smothers, Nicole Eugene, and Virginia McFadden. 2009. "Archiving the Voices and Needs of Katrina's Children: The Uses and Importance of Stories Narrated Survivor-to-Survivor." In *Children, Law, and Disasters: What We Have Learned from the Hurricanes of 2005*, edited by American Bar Association, 61–112. Chicago: American Bar Association; Houston: University of Houston.

Lindahl, Carl, and Susan G. Nash. 2008. "Survivor-to-Survivor Storytelling and Trauma Recovery." *The Dialogue: A Quarterly Technical Assistance Bulletin on Disaster Behavioral Health* 5 (1): 11–13.

Malcolm, Noel. 2016. "Passions for the Past: The Aubrey Story." *New York Review of Books*, December 8, 2016, 36–38.

McNamara, Dallas [Alice G.], Pat Jasper, and Carl Lindahl. 2007–9. *Who We Are*. Interactive photographic and audio installation. Displayed at Art League Houston, Project Row Houses, and Rice University, Houston, Texas; and the Carver Museum, Austin, Texas. A miniaturized version of the installation is accessible online at http://www .houstonculture.org/houston/SKRHphotos.html.

Pennebaker, James A., ed. 1995. *Emotion, Disclosure, and Health*. Washington, DC: American Psychological Association.

———. 1997. *Opening Up: The Healing Power of Expressing Emotions*. 2nd ed. New York: Guilford.

Scurr, Ruth. 2015. *John Aubrey, My Own Life*. London: Chatto & Windus.

Shuman, Amy. 2006. "Entitlement and Empathy in Personal Narrative." *Narrative Inquiry* 16 (1): 148–55.

Smith, Carl. 1995. *Urban Disorder and the Shape of Belief: The Great Chicago Fire, the Haymarket Bomb, and the Model Town of Pullman*. Chicago: University of Chicago Press.

Solnit, Rebecca. 2009. *A Paradise Built in Hell: The Extraordinary Communities That Arise in Disaster*. New York: Viking.

The Sphere Project. 2011. *Humanitarian Charter and Minimum Standards in Humanitarian Response*. 3rd ed. Rugby: Practical Action.

Terkel, Studs. 1984. *The Good War: An Oral History of World War II*. New York: Pantheon.

Tran, Mai. 2005. "Houston Mall Is a Lifeline for Vietnamese Who Fled." *Los Angeles Times*, September 6, 2005. https://www.latimes.com/archives/la-xpm-2005-sep-06-me-vietnam6-story.html.

Vanlandingham, Mark J. 2015. "Post-Katrina, Vietnamese Success." *New York Times*, August 14, 2015. http://www.nytimes.com/2015/08/16/opinion/sunday/post-katrina-vietnamese-success.html.

Vollen, Lola, and Chris Ying, eds. 2006. *Voices from the Storm: The People of New Orleans on Hurricane Katrina and Its Aftermath*. San Francisco: McSweeney's.

Carl LINDAHL is Martha Gano Houstoun Research Professor in English at the University of Houston, cofounder of the disaster response project Surviving Katrina and Rita in Houston, and founder of the earthquake response project *Memwa Ayisyen* /Haitian Memory. His books include (with B. J. Ancelet and M. Gaudet) *Second Line Rescue: Improvised Responses to Katrina and Rita* (2013).

2

INTO THE BULLRING

The Significance of "Empathy" after the Earthquake

Yutaka Suga

ON MARCH 11, 2011, A TRAGEDY—THE GREAT EAST Japan Earthquake— struck the coast of Japan's Tohoku region. The massive earthquake occurred off the Pacific coast and caused a tsunami on an unimaginable scale, taking more than eighteen thousand lives and erasing entire communities from the ground. Following the disaster, the Japanese government launched a large-scale recovery project, scheduled to last five years and expected to cost a massive $250 billion. Engaged in the public works resulting from this recovery effort are not only swarms of construction and other private companies but also vast numbers of researchers and experts involved in recovery planning and so-called survey activities supporting such planning.

My goal is not simply to criticize the researchers and experts who flocked to and may still be active in the disaster-affected region for continuing to selfishly profit from the sweet nectar that comes with disaster. In fact, the majority of researchers and experts were, or are, probably engaged in survey and research activities related to recovery efforts intended to help the survivors. Furthermore, the arrival of these researchers and experts certainly was seen as encouraging and actually saved struggling communities and survivors. That said, there were also undoubtedly researchers and experts who, under the guise of projects aimed at helping survivors, exploited those affected by disaster and themselves profited from the recovery effort. It is also possible that even research and activities intended to help survivors, on closer inspection, did not end up benefiting them.[1]

In 2005, the southern United States was struck by Hurricane Katrina. Amid the confusion in the immediate aftermath of the disaster, some extremely predatory economic measures were put in place. Naomi Klein criticized such conditions—in which power is used to change society while citizens are still suffering from an overwhelming sense of insecurity following a social crisis—labeling it the "shock doctrine" (Klein 2007). The term refers to the mindset in which the recovery process following a major calamity is seen as an unparalleled market opportunity and to the application of a market fundamentalism to devastating effect under such circumstances. This can alternatively be called a kind of "disaster capitalism" based on exploitation of major disasters (Klein 2007, 6). To certain people with power wishing to implement radical policies, the social instability triggered by shocking events or threats is a propitious opportunity.[2] While Japan is being attacked in the same manner by disaster capitalism following the Great East Japan Earthquake, it is also threatened by "research" and "activities" that similarly exploit major disasters.

In this chapter, I explore, on the basis of my own experiences, the attitudes and methods that folklorists should employ when interacting with survivors in a disaster-affected area. In 2004, seven years prior to the Great East Japan Earthquake of 2011, my long-term field site—the Higashiyama area of Ojiya City in Niigata Prefecture—became a disaster-affected region after being struck by an earthquake, the so-called Chūetsu-Niigata Earthquake, transforming my "subjects" into "survivors." As a result of the disaster, my own survey and research methods, my attitude as a researcher when relating to my subjects, and my feelings toward them all changed. Immediately following the earthquake, as a symbol of recovery, survivors in my research field began to employ a cultural tradition that they had maintained over the years. Numerous researchers and experts besides myself participated in this process, but as a folklorist I began to feel uncomfortable with their activities. Instead I decided to find my own way of participating and interacting with the survivors. Based on this experience, in the pages that follow I discuss the significance and need for folklorists and ethnographers to have empathy toward survivors in times of disaster.

A Field Site Affected by an Earthquake Disaster

Over the past two hundred years, the practice of bullfighting has been passed down from generation to generation in the intermountain villages of the Higashiyama area.³ I began fieldwork in this region in 1998, as part of my research on traditional culture. However, on October 23, 2004, a near-field magnitude 6.8 earthquake struck. In this region, located directly above the hypocenter of the earthquake, precious lives were lost, along with the majority of houses and properties. Bulls and the tradition of bullfighting were also lost.⁴ To the people of this area, the loss of a bull raised within the family caused the same grief as would the death of a family member.

As an ethnographer, prior to the earthquake I conducted research based on impartial and objective observation of the culture and inhabitants of the region. I did not have any reservations about perceiving and interacting with the inhabitants as informants. My job, after all, was to be objective. As a result of the earthquake, however, I could no longer consider the inhabitants simply to be informants. I began to develop a relationship in which I thought, experienced, and felt sadness and joy together with them. An insensitive researcher might deride me for unabashedly admitting this and criticize me for being naive and intoxicated with a lukewarm sentimentality. There is no doubt in my mind, however, that it is because of this deep personal relationship that I was able to understand the significance of the loss of both people and bulls to the community. Of course, I did not deepen my relationships for the purpose of gaining such understanding. It just happened as a matter of course.

I managed somehow to reach the disaster-affected area ten days after the earthquake, at a time when public transportation had not yet been resumed. On arrival, I began to look for friends and acquaintances who had been evacuated. They had taken refuge in a school gymnasium with only the barest necessities. The gymnasium was overflowing with survivors, all of whom were completely exhausted. It was there that, despite these dire circumstances, I witnessed a truly surprising scene: my friends who had survived the disaster were gathered in a corner discussing how to continue the tradition of bullfighting. In the midst of aftershocks, I would have expected my friends, who had just lost their homes, possessions, and jobs, to be focused only on how they would survive from this point forward. Yet remarkably, even in such painful circumstances, they continued to think about bullfighting. Later, they would proactively adopt the cultural tradition of bullfighting as a symbol for the region's recovery from the earthquake and, in fact, use it as a driving force for recovery. And as their hometown and bullfighting were restored, many inhabitants would return to the area.

I participated in such efforts to restore the region using cultural traditions. My involvement, however, was not the kind of proactive intervention based on extrinsic values or off-the-shelf methods typically employed by experts or applied researchers. Rather, it was relatively passive and involved staying close by and listening to survivors, identifying the values they considered important, and providing my expertise only when asked to do so. It is likely that experts and scholars focused on action and response would find my activity to be insufficient. However, I intentionally decided to develop an approach that was qualitatively different from the one taken by such experts and scholars.

The Onslaught of Outside Professionals

Prior to the earthquake, I was the only person with the title of scholar or professor who visited the Higashiyama area. This area did not have any outstanding features, and, other than for a few folklorists interested in bullfighting, it did not seem to hold any particular appeal as a field site for scholars or experts in general. However, the region's value as a field site shifted 180 degrees as a result of the earthquake: all kinds of outside professionals—including scholars and their students; nonprofit organizations (NPOs); governmental consultants; and government officials—flocked to the area and, after identifying bullfighting as a cultural resource, began various recovery projects centered on this tradition. Among such professionals, there were some who claimed to be conducting research to support regional recovery but who, in fact, were using the region as a testing ground and exploiting the survivors to further their own research objectives. In addition, there were professionals who attempted to gain access to funds intended for the recovery by associating themselves with the recovery effort.

In general, experts and individuals working within the public sector have a thorough knowledge of various social systems and institutions and possess nearly monopolistic skills for their usage. Put simply, knowledge regarding the source of recovery funds, an understanding of the process for accessing such funds, and the specialized skills required for planning are in the hands of only a certain group of experts. Laypeople do not possess the knowledge or skills required to access necessary resources. For this reason, they have no choice but to rely on experts—or at least are made to believe they have no choice. The recovery projects implemented in the Higashiyama area were typically rife with such structural problems.

Certain governmental consultants received commissions, paid from the recovery money, for designing recovery projects. To increase their commissions, the consultants would expand the scope of their projects, claiming that such expansions were warranted because of requests from survivors. These consultants and cooperating NPOs held a total of twenty workshops and meetings in Higashiyama to hear such requests. On the surface, this may appear to be an ideal example of collaboration in which various actors—including experts, scholars, NPOs, governmental agencies, and local community members—met frequently to exchange opinions and establish a division of labor. While it is certain that the voices of residents were picked up as a result of these meetings, it is also certain that these voices were generated within the fixed dichotomized structure of researcher/researched, professional/nonprofessional, and supporter/supported. Regardless of how freely the survivors were allowed to speak, it was the consultants who prepared the questions prior to the meeting and who led the discussions. In the formal context of workshops and meetings, the people of Higashiyama struggled to formulate formal-sounding narratives that differed from the content of everyday conversation. The workshops, which were dressed up to seem like a natural way to pick up survivors' requests, were, in fact, unnatural interviews guided to conform to the expectations of the consultants and others. For example, one consultant came up with a plan, which normally would not have been thought feasible, to build a domed bullfighting ring that could be used during rain and which would cost several million dollars. The proposal was based on an offhand comment by a survivor talking about a dream stadium—naturally, the plan was never adopted. Even after this particular plan evaporated, consultants continued to propose one new recovery project after another for the next few years.

From the perspective of the consultants, the job was to generate revenue; expanding the scale of projects was one way to facilitate this. In the case of subsidies and grants, however, the beneficiaries are generally responsible for covering a portion of the project cost; in other words, the expansion of a project means increasing the proportion for which the local community is responsible. The people of Higashiyama were well aware of this arrangement but had to remain silent because they could not access the funds necessary to restore bullfighting and their lives without being a part of projects managed by outside professionals.

As the recovery process continued, I began to feel uncomfortable about the attitudes and relationships created by these professionals. At the same time, I became keenly aware of the need to approach participation in recovery activities from a different standpoint and employ different methods. I had visited the area many times prior to the earthquake and had already developed a rapport with the survivors. Furthermore, as a folklorist, I had a deep understanding of the culture and values of the area. As I continued to visit after the earthquake to listen to the experiences of survivors, I developed empathy for them and began to feel their agony—which I had not directly experienced myself—as my own. It was during this process that I became increasingly uncomfortable about the involvement and methods used by many of the outside professionals. Ultimately, I decided to participate in recovery activities from the standpoint of the survivors.

My Changes, Changes Experienced by the Survivors

The research methods I used in the field changed dramatically after I became involved in the recovery effort. I hardly ever took out my field notebook, IC recorder, or camera, all of which I had used extensively until that point. Whenever survivors would talk about their tragic experiences, it was not as part of an interview but rather as part of normal conversation. In addition, I was allowed to become a member of the organization in charge of bullfighting. That is how I came to stand in the bullfighting ring as a bullfighter myself and came to own a bull named Tenjin. This was not simply a case of participant observation to study the finer points of bullfighting culture. Rather, it was a way to partially gain the legitimacy necessary to intervene in the culture by developing a deeper understanding of survivors' thoughts and feelings and by gaining partial entitlement as a tradition bearer. That said, I did not intentionally plan to become a tradition bearer. It would be better to say that this was the natural result of the reciprocal interaction between my empathy for the survivors and their acceptance thereof.

After becoming a member of the bullfighting organization, I attempted to assert to my bullfighting comrades that the recovery projects underway were being exploited by outside professionals, that such reliance on outside professionals should be stopped, and that they should try to actualize recovery projects on their own. I use the term *assert* here, but these were not opinions expressed in formal settings such as meetings or workshops, as would typically be the case for an outside professional. Rather, they were comments made in informal contexts. For example, if the topic of recovery projects were to come up at a feast after a bullfight, I might express my opinion as one of the boys. At first glance, some might consider such a method of communication to be passive and ineffective. However, from my previous interactions with the survivors, I had learned that, in this region, it was important to express opinions through such informal dialogue. Although opinions expressed in informal, everyday conversations do not have any direct or clear impact, they have an indirect and unconscious effect on people's decision-making.

Of course, as a member of the organization in charge of bullfighting, I was also entitled to express my views in formal discussions on recovery activities. Furthermore, I additionally had the opportunity to influence leaders of the organization with whom I had close relationships. However, I hesitated to take this direct approach. I feared that my title of professor, from which I could not escape, would take on a certain authority in formal settings. If a person such as myself, having the authority of a scholar, were to say something in an official setting, the comments could have excessive influence on the local community's decision-making and prevent people from expressing their true views.[5] Therefore, my only choice was to continue to softly convince the survivors in informal settings about the problematic aspects of recovery activities that rely so heavily on outside actors.

As time passed, the survivors became increasingly frustrated with the growing financial burden resulting from projects designed by outside professionals and the absurdity of outside professionals benefiting from commissions as a result of such projects. Their dissatisfaction was further aggravated by the fact that the values embedded in the cultural traditions they had maintained for so long were not respected in the projects designed by outsiders. Ultimately this led the community members to sever their dependence on outside professionals and to develop plans independently, becoming the central drivers of their own recovery activities.

Subsequently, survivors began negotiating with the government themselves. Officers of the bullfighting organization frequently visited municipal offices, studied the schemes and application processes for accessing recovery funds, gathered information from regional politicians, and collected donations from influential individuals in the local community. Other members of the organization contributed to such activities however they could. Some members offered their land as sites for cattle barns, while other members used their skills to, for example, remove trees that were in the way. Eventually, I too was included in this organically occurring division of labor. They expected me to use my specialist knowledge and skills as a folklorist with the title of university professor. As such, I was assigned the task of preparing official documents necessary to acquire external funds and of communicating with the mass media about the importance of traditional culture. These were not roles that I had proactively offered to the survivors. They were roles assigned to me as a result of the trust that had developed as community residents got to know me through our mutual enjoyment of bullfighting and my expression of empathy for their experiences. Other survivors were assigned a wide variety of roles. In this context, mine was just one role among many.

Asymptotic Relationship: A Positionality That Precludes Identifying Completely with Subjects

It goes without saying that I am an outsider just the same as other outside professionals. I am well aware that no matter how deeply or how long I interact with the people of the region, I can never identify completely with them. Furthermore, I also believe that it is better for me not to naively think that I can identify with them. It is an asymptotic relationship in which I can approach but never be the same as them. I believe, however, that even if it is not possible for ethnographers to identify with their subjects completely, it is important that they try to get closer to them. We need to first recognize that no matter how close we get or how much empathy we have for a certain group, regardless of what group that is, we can never totally identify with its members. And, on the basis of this recognition, we must continue to get closer to our subjects and thereby gain a deeper understanding of their thinking and values. This approach based on empathy constitutes a challenge to share, at least partially, the context in which the subjects find themselves, as well as their emotions and their perceptions. And it constitutes a challenge to obtain entitlement in this process by understanding, thinking, speaking, and acting from the perspective of the subjects.

Although outside professionals and scholars flocked to the disaster-affected region following the Chūetsu-Niigata Earthquake in 2004, their numbers declined over time. Today, almost two decades after the disaster, the outside professionals, consultants, and NPOs that once swarmed to Higashiyama are nowhere to be found. Their jobs are done. By disappearing, they have avoided direct exposure to the consequences and the evaluation of their actions by the local community. Having become a participant in bullfighting, however, I have no end point. My destiny as a bull owner and as a tradition bearer is for my work to continue to be evaluated for the rest of my life.

One day, after the majority of outside professionals had left Higashiyama, a member of the local community said to me, "You didn't bring a single cent to the community but you're still here." This was the greatest compliment I could have received. What this expresses, without saying it explicitly, is the importance of continuing to share experiences with the community, here and now. Through my involvement in the recovery process following the earthquake, I have become aware of the need for research and intervention methods based on relationships without a set end date, research that is not fixed, normative, standardized, generic, or conducted for a certain purpose or toward a certain a priori goal.

Empathetic Scholars

While it is inevitable that the research and activities of ethnographers will have some impact on their subjects, this impact reflexively returns to the ethnographers themselves. We must be aware that such reflexivity has the potential to dramatically alter a scholar's positionality and ideology, as well as their methods, objectives, and research content. To exclude such potential from the start creates bias. It is entirely natural for an ethnographer, as a human being, to develop empathy for others. Indeed, it is an attitude of *not denying empathy* that is expected of an ethnographer.

It is perhaps necessary here to explore the term *empathy* in greater depth. To do so requires drawing a contrast with the term *sympathy*. The two terms are not always mutually exclusive, but on closer inspection they are quite different. Sympathy is an act of emotional expression such as compassion or concern that involves emotionally aligning with or agreeing with another person. It can easily lead to feelings of pity toward those weaker or inferior to oneself. In contrast, empathy, while also being an act of emotional expression, involves an active attempt to enter another's inner world and to understand them by projecting a part of oneself. The utility of empathy lies in this understanding.

Empathy is a translation of the German *Einfühlung*, a term that enjoyed widespread usage in the late nineteenth and early twentieth centuries in the disciplines of aesthetics, philosophy, and psychology and was a key concept in the *Phänomenologie* proposed by the Austrian philosopher Edmund

Gustav Albrecht Husserl. The English translation of the term, *empathy*, was also widely adopted in English-speaking countries, where it underwent a unique evolution of its own. For example, *empathy* was employed as an important analytical concept and key word in the highly popular "Self Psychology" proposed by Heinz Kohut.[6]

Kohut (1984, 82) defines the word as follows: "The best definition of empathy—the analogue to my terse scientific definition of empathy as 'vicarious introspection'—is that it is the capacity to think and feel oneself into the inner life of another person. It is our lifelong ability to experience what another person experiences, though usually, and appropriately, to an attenuated degree." Empathy is "vicarious introspection" or, more simply, one person's attempt to experience the inner life of another while simultaneously retaining the stance of an objective observer (175).

Although the concept of empathy as defined by Kohut carries with it multifaceted and complicated implications, for the purposes of this chapter I suggest a simplified interpretation of empathy as "a method for putting oneself in another's inner life in order to feel, experience, and understand" their world. A notable feature of such a conceptualization is that it avoids overly simplistic identification with the other. One's experience of the subject's world is attenuated to a certain degree—it is less intense than the other person's experience. Furthermore, while one attempts to experience the other's inner life, one does so from one's own positionality. Insofar as empathy allows one to understand not only another's negative experiences, such as sadness and anger, but also positive experiences such as joy and pleasure, its scope is much greater than that of the compassion and pity that are a part of sympathy. Through my bullfighting activities, I was able to share not only the survivors' painful experiences following the earthquake but also their everyday joys. Empathy can be thought of as a method that allows us to cross the boundaries of positionality to more deeply understand the full range of human emotions.[7]

Conclusions

The research and activities of scholars and outside professionals in disaster-affected areas appear to suffer from an empathy deficit. For example, many of these people, including folklorists, have conducted interview surveys with survivors of the Great East Japan Earthquake—including with residents whose wounds are still open—with the stated goal of using the experiences of this earthquake to improve our response to future disasters. Among such scholars, there are some who fail to consider the current emotional and psychological state of the survivors. There are also researchers who wield their status, authority, or relationship with the government to exploit disaster-affected areas as testing grounds and use survivors as guinea pigs to further their own research agendas.[8] Despite lacking true empathy, such scholars typically act, at least superficially, as if they are motivated by empathy. They often cause survivors, who have already been wounded by natural disaster, to experience secondary (human-made) suffering. In order to avoid causing such secondary suffering, and to prevent other scholars from causing it as well, ethnographers must maintain close relationships and develop true empathy with their subjects.

I must mention here that if scholars and outside professionals develop an excessive degree of empathy, problems similar to those resulting from a deficit of empathy can arise. When outside scholars and professionals become emotionally involved with survivors but do not develop the requisite understanding, there is a risk they will fall into self-righteous empathy. The closer one gets to the survivors, the more one feels (perhaps baselessly) and acts as if identifying with them. There is a chance in such a situation that the outsider's intentions will not match the perceptions, emotions, goals, and methods desired by the survivors themselves. Decisions made by individuals who believe they are in sync with the survivors may, in fact, have unwanted consequences. For example, following the Chūetsu-Niigata Earthquake in 2004 and Great East Japan Earthquake in 2011, massive amounts of supplies were sent from around the country to shelters where large numbers of evacuees had assembled. A major proportion of these supplies, however, comprised items that the survivors either could not use or did not need, and this ultimately hindered the delivery of emergency supplies. This problem was caused by self-righteous empathy, which, like an empathy deficit, can further harm survivors.

Amy Shuman (2006, 152–53) points out the potential problem of empathy: "Empathy offers the possibility of understanding across space and time, but it rarely changes the circumstances of those who suffer. If it provides inspiration, it is more often for those in the privileged position of empathizer rather than empathized." Unless one is vigilant, empathy can mutate into self-righteous empathy or something similar to sympathy.

The term *empathy*, whose meaning encompasses the understanding of others, appears to be more rational than *sympathy*. Accordingly, scholars who are concerned with empathy as a means of understanding others undoubtedly make an effort to remain calm, collected, and objective. In practice, however, they may not always be able to maintain this calm, objective stance. Although they may attempt to experience the inner world of others without disrupting their own sentiments (emotions), in reality, the closer they are to their subjects, the more their own sentiments are influenced and the greater the likelihood that they will fall into the kind of sentimental sympathy and self-righteous empathy that should be avoided. Ethnographers who act from the standpoint of survivors must become sensitive to such potential problems associated with empathy and must remain self-reflective. Scholars who empathize run the risk of having their emotions take over, and of descending into self-righteousness or narcissism.

That said, I want to emphasize the point that even if such potential risks exist, there is no need to avoid research and activities based on empathy. For a long time, in the context of research and related activities, we have forced ourselves to try to remain objective and, as much as possible, to pin down facts. Scholars and professionals have tended to undervalue empathy as an emotional capacity and an emotional act. In times of crisis following disasters, however, it is necessary to pay attention to such emotional aspects and take them into consideration. Empathy is also a powerful means by which to counter research and activities that take advantage of disasters. What is important is not simply to feel what the survivors feel but, rather, to more accurately and more deeply understand the thinking, values, and wishes of the survivors. By correctly understanding and correctly transmitting the thinking of survivors to the broader society, folklorists capable of empathy can contribute substantially to communities struck by disasters.

Afterword, Added in 2021

I own a fighting bull named Tenjin. He turned seventeen this year but still enters the bullring to fight. A few years ago, I injured my spine in an accident in the bullring and was hospitalized for three weeks, but I have made a comeback as a bullfighter and still enjoy the thrill of the bullring along with Tenjin. Not only do I continue bullfighting, but I have also been using my expertise as a folklorist to work with the local people in a collaborative effort to pass on, maintain, and create "tradition."

Currently, the tradition of bullfighting is being subjected to modern logic and values, as well as the influence of outside institutions and resources, such as concern for animal welfare and questions about the tradition's gender restrictions (only men may participate in bullfighting), efforts to protect an intangible cultural heritage, and the development of tourism and of the region as a whole. Therefore, it is important that we fully understand the circumstances of a tradition even as we endeavor to carry it on. To this end, the local bullfighters and I decided to undertake a collaborative project to improve our understanding of the increasingly complex external factors and the social mechanisms that drive them so that we might enhance our ability to respond appropriately. We have been holding various study sessions to help us develop the ability to resist outside interventions that tend to ignore local logic, while also improving our skills in utilizing the outside institutions and resources that are essential for sustaining local traditions. For example, we have studied the laws and regulations pertaining to animal welfare and Japan's programs for protecting intangible cultural heritage. We have also held a session in which women, who tend to be reticent, were given the opportunity to speak to the gender issue inherent in the bullfighting tradition. Other activities include building networks and providing opportunities for the exchange of opinions with people involved in bullfighting in other regions. In the midst of all of this, I have purposely remained passive, only assisting if asked. Nevertheless, I do believe there are roles we can fulfill as folklorists, and that is when I morph from bullfighter to specialist.

Notes

1. On March 10, 2012, one year after the Great East Japan Earthquake, a graduate student in sociology posted on her personal blog some critical comments regarding the damage so-called research activities were causing in disaster-affected areas. In response to the disaster, she had decided to take a leave of absence from her graduate studies in Tokyo and return home to Miyagi Prefecture (which had been strongly affected by the disaster) to support recovery efforts and conduct field research. It was then that she courageously sounded the alarm about the selfish surveys and activities of scholars and outside professionals who did not understand the survivors (Yamauchi 2012).

2. As the government and other influential parties were attempting to cleverly exploit the hurricane damage to their own advantage, a group of folklorists initiated a project using their skills to support the survivors of the hurricane. In 2005, Carl Lindahl and Pat Jasper started a survivor-centered storytelling and documentation project titled Surviving Katrina and Rita in Houston. Reports of the project (Lindahl 2006, 2012) were introduced in Japan after the Great East Japan Earthquake, greatly influencing the behavior of Japanese folklorists responding to disasters.

3. In the West, the term *bullfighting* generally evokes images of a bullfight that pits human against bull, similar to traditions found in Spain. Bullfighting as practiced throughout East Asia, however, is typically bull versus bull. The uniqueness of Ojiya bullfighting, the subject of my own study, lies in the fact that a draw can be called in the middle of the fight. As bulls in this region have traditionally been considered members of the family, they are well cared for on a daily basis. Furthermore, in comparison to bullfighting as practiced in other regions, the owners have a higher awareness of protecting their animals (Suga 2013). In 1978, Ojiya bullfighting was designated by the Japanese government to be an "important intangible folk cultural property" (*jūyō mukei minzoku bunkazai*).

4. As a result of this earthquake, 68 individuals, primarily the elderly and children, lost their lives in Ojiya City, Tokamachi City, Nagaoka City, Mitsuke City, and surrounding areas. Another 4,805 individuals were injured, and, at the peak, approximately 103,000 residents were living as evacuees. Approximately seventeen thousand houses were destroyed. Of the ninety-seven bulls being raised in the area, twenty were lost because of collapsed barns and similar causes.

5. The people of this region are not used to voicing their opinions or asserting themselves in formal settings. Instead, they frankly and proactively express their views in informal, everyday conversations, and it is through such conversations that consensus is achieved. Negotiation, as traditionally practiced in the local community, does not take place in meetings but, rather, through repeated dialogue in everyday settings. I simply adopted this approach as well. However, such methods for achieving consensus embedded in the local culture were overlooked by the majority of outside researchers and professionals. In fact, such an approach to negotiation would have been considered inconvenient, given their desire to retain control of projects.

6. The English term *empathy* itself is relatively new. It was first proposed by the British psychologist Edward Bradford Titchener as a translation of the German *Einfühlung* (Titchener 1909a, 1909b).

7. Amy Shuman (2006, 149) argues that "empathy appropriates the personal with the goal of greater understanding across experiential differences." Empathy is an emotional act that, while potentially developing into self-righteousness, can lead to clearer understanding of others' experiences, personal values, and thinking.

8. In terms of Japanese folkloristics, after the earthquake the Agency for Cultural Affairs and other governmental entities funded salvage folklore projects in which folklorists and cultural anthropologists were mobilized to assess damage and protect cultural assets. However, such investigations have not necessarily been implemented with sufficient consideration of the dire circumstances in which survivors find themselves. The majority of folklorists are interested in festivals and rites that are at risk of being lost as a result of an earthquake disaster; even as they stand face to face with survivors, folklorists tend to ignore the difficulties experienced by them in their daily lives.

References

Klein, Naomi. 2007. *The Shock Doctrine: The Rise of Disaster Capitalism*. New York: Picador.

Kohut, Heinz. 1984. *How Does Analysis Cure?* Chicago: University of Chicago Press.

Lindahl, Carl. 2006. "Storms of Memory: New Orleanians Surviving Katrina in Houston."
    Callaloo 29 (4): 1526–38.

———. 2012. "Legends of Hurricane Katrina: The Right to Be Wrong, Survivor-to-Survivor
    Storytelling, and Healing." *Journal of American Folklore* 125 (496): 139–76.

Shuman, Amy. 2006. "Entitlement and Empathy in Personal Narrative." *Narrative Inquiry*
    16 (1): 148–55.

Suga Yutaka. 2013. *"Atarashii no no gakumon" no jidai e: Chishiki seisan to shakai jissen o
    tsunagu tame ni*. Tokyo: Iwanami Shoten.

Titchener, Edward Bradford. 1909a. *Elementary Psychology of the Thought Processes*. New
    York: Macmillan.

———. 1909b. *A Text-Book of Psychology*. New York: Macmillan.

Yamauchi Akemi. 2012. "Akademizumu ga shokku dokutorin?" *Date burogu* (blog), March
    10, 2012. http://akemi.da-te.jp/e477644.html.

Yutaka SUGA is Professor of Folkloristics at the University of Tokyo. He is author of *Atarashii no no gakumon no jidai e: Chishiki seisan to shakai jissen o tsunagu tame ni* (Toward a new era in grassroots scholarship: Linking knowledge production and social practice; 2013).

3

REBUILDING AND RECONNECTING AFTER DISASTER

Listening to Older Adults

Yoko Taniguchi

NATURAL DISASTERS, SUCH AS EARTHQUAKES, FLOODS, VOLCANIC ERUP-tions, tornadoes, and storms, occur frequently in Japan. Every disaster differs in scale and complexity, and disasters cannot simply be compared to one another in terms of losses or casualties. If one were to attempt such a comparison, however, the Great East Japan Earthquake of March 11, 2011, would be considered the third most catastrophic natural disaster to cause tremendous damage in Japan (Ushiyama 2012, 5). It would follow only the Great Kanto Earthquake of September 1, 1923, which resulted in an enormous number of human casualties, and the Meiji Sanriku Earthquake of June 15, 1896, which affected nearly the same tsunami-prone coastal zones in the Tohoku region as the 2011 earthquake.

In light of the large number of natural disasters that have affected Japan in the past, Japanese government authorities, at both local and national levels, have established an elaborate public assistance system. People have developed autonomous mutual assistance systems in their respective communities. And Japanese social and natural scientists have advanced theories and conducted research not only on ways of preventing or mitigating disasters but also on ways of rebuilding social relationships and creating new cultures revolving around disaster.

As an ethnographer, my work has involved conducting fieldwork with older adults who were affected by the 6.8 magnitude Chūetsu-Niigata

Earthquake that occurred on October 23, 2004, in the Niigata Prefecture region. (For other experiences with the 2004 Chūetsu-Niigata Earthquake, see chap. 2.) I wanted to explore how these residents expressed their feelings about the event and their subsequent experiences of displacement as they were forced to leave their hometowns. My study, which used participant-observation and interview techniques, began in late 2008. I interviewed current and former residents of Yamakoshi, a rural mountain village made up of fourteen districts with close-knit neighborhoods.

The 2004 earthquake destroyed the main road connecting the village to the wider world. Fortunately, only a few inhabitants sustained injury, but their houses suffered severe damage, and residents had no choice but to evacuate the village until its infrastructure was restored. They took refuge in purpose-built temporary housing located in a district about one hour's drive from Yamakoshi. Some of the villagers lived in these temporary accommodations for up to three and a half years. The year 2014 marked the tenth anniversary of the earthquake, and the village has moved into the third phase of disaster recovery, which means the damaged infrastructure and houses have been restored, residents' daily lives are back on track, and various community revitalization activities have been launched. It has been well over a decade since I first became involved with the village and its residents.

This is a case study of how people tell stories about reconnecting with their hometowns after disaster and about the long-term displacement that has upset the foundations of their lives. I explore these issues by analyzing narratives I collected in interviews with adults over the age of sixty. In the pages that follow, I first describe the way in which the residents and I have built relationships. Second, I present a regional outline of the village, describing its geography, its population, its history, and the aftermath of the 2004 earthquake. Third, I detail the processes involved in the residents' displacement, and their lives in temporary housing. Lastly, by examining their narratives, I explore the primary factors that influenced the survivors' decisions to return to their hometown and restart their daily lives.

Beginning the Interview Process: Building a Rapport with Interviewees

I first met the residents of the village in late December 2008, when the temporary housing district where they were sheltered was about to be closed.

I was there as an ethnographer, but I had an opportunity to participate as a volunteer in one of the support activities assigned by the disaster volunteer center. I was tasked with helping a family carry boxes from their temporary accommodation to their original home, which had been repaired after being damaged in the earthquake. While participating in this activity, I did not think it was appropriate to use my camera, voice recorder, pen, and notebook in the presence of the residents; however, the ethnographer in me still strove to engrave on my memory everything I saw and heard.

Following this volunteer work, I began the interview process. My first interview was carried out with staff members of the disaster volunteer center. I also spoke to the landlady of the guesthouse I stayed in and the chair of one of the neighborhood associations. The guesthouse, which was formerly the general store, was opened during the early stages of the disaster recovery operation to provide food and lodging for workers involved in the reconstruction of buildings and roads. During the interviews, people informed me about life within the temporary housing district following displacement. Interviewees also told me about their family, friends, and neighbors.

Before I actually began my fieldwork, I had figured that it might take time for interviewees to feel comfortable sharing their experiences and feelings with me. This belief was bolstered by the fact that I had never directly experienced a catastrophic disaster or displacement myself and also by the fact that I was a stranger from outside the community. But the situation was not as I anticipated. Over the past years, the people I have interviewed have willingly shared their time and their company with me. They have treated me as if I were one of their young friends. A woman in her sixties, who provided me with accommodation during my fieldwork over the last few years, told me one day that she felt as if I were her own daughter. This feeling might have been triggered by the fact that I am about the same age as her children, but it certainly developed as we grew closer and closer over time.

In our first interview, the woman told me a story about life during the period of displacement and the effects of mutual help. When the time came to end the interview, I expressed my gratitude to her and closed my notebook. Before I could finish, however, she suddenly started telling me, without being asked, how she felt about the fact that the village was still labeled "the disaster area" and the residents were still called "the victims," even after they had returned to their homes or moved to new places to restart their daily lives. She told me that she felt uncomfortable with these labels and that she just wanted to live in the village quietly.

When I heard her telling me this, I thought it would be a challenge for me, as both a person and an ethnographer, to continue with my interviews in this village. I decided to tell her about my own anxieties and my motivations for doing this sort of interview about personal disaster experiences. I feared that my requests for interviews might hurt the people who had been devastated by the earthquake and who had already answered so many questions about it.

This fear was related to my status as an "outsider," both as a nonlocal resident and in terms of the disaster experience. At the same time, of course, natural disasters are totally unpredictable and could happen at any time, at any place, and to anyone. This was, therefore, as much my own concern as anyone else's. I told the woman that my sense of mission both as a person and as an ethnographer motivated me to transmit the stories and lessons I collected to a wider audience. I also told her that stories of the mutual help practiced among the residents would act as important and powerful messages for future generations and for people who have not experienced such disasters. She listened to me silently before saying that she now had a sense of mission as a person with disaster experience and that she agreed with what I had just said. She told me she had always wanted to do something in return for the kindness shown by people from all over Japan. For her, letting people know that the residents of the village had become healthy and happy was a good way to achieve this.

Following our conversation, we grew closer to each other. I also realized that my worries about the potential communication difficulties between the respondents and me were, in the end, unfounded. Former interviewees were kind enough to introduce me to new interviewees, and the experience mentioned above also helped me build relations with other people in the community who could share their stories with me.

Most of my interviewees had lived in the village until the earthquake struck, and their family houses, yards, and graves had stood there for generations. Most of them have returned to their original homes now, but some decided to move on and live elsewhere. The interviews were conducted in their homes. I tried to create an atmosphere in which the speaker would feel comfortable; I started, for example, with a few simple questions about everyday life, especially about their families. Once I was assured that they were ready to discuss their disaster experiences, I started to ask questions.[1] During the early interviews, which were conducted about three years after the earthquake, they often told stories about how they had helped one another during the emergency situation. After four or five years, the focus of their stories had shifted to their sense of belonging to their hometown.

Displacement and Life in Temporary Housing

Yamakoshi, the hometown village of my interviewees, is located in an area of heavy snows, surrounded by mountains. Sparsely populated and rural, the village comprises fourteen districts and is distinguished by a culture known for bullfighting and raising carp. Traditionally the main industries were agriculture, sericulture, and charcoal production, but in the 1920s, a number of teenage girls migrated to the area to work in the spinning mills as wage laborers. From the 1960s through the 1970s, many young men moved to the cities to earn higher wages that they could remit to their families. Since that time, the village has gradually depopulated, a trend that was accelerated by the 2004 earthquake: the population of 2,083 people and 672 households before the disaster decreased to 1,325 people and 487 households in its aftermath. The population of village residents over the age of sixty-five increased from 30 percent to 40 percent, while the Japanese national average was 25 percent as of 2014.

The earthquake on October 23, 2004, with a magnitude of 6.8 and a seismic intensity of 5, caused significant landslides. One of the survivors explained how she felt when the earthquake struck: "My three-story house with a concrete foundation, which was built just two months before the earthquake, shook so that it resembled a diamond when the earthquake struck" (Taniguchi 2010). Long afterward, residents remained sensitive to even small tremors: they remembered the earthquake with their bodies.

Two days after the earthquake, everybody was evacuated from the mountains to the city by a helicopter dispatched by the Self-Defense Forces. For two months, the displaced residents lived in a gymnasium. They were then relocated to new temporary housing built on vacant land in an urban area one hour's drive from their hometown. This temporary housing district was established on 3.5 acres of hills in a section of the city that had been constructed in the mid-1970s. The displaced residents lived there for up to three years, during which time access to their hometown remained restricted because of the risk of secondary disasters.

The temporary housing district consisted not only of accommodations but also of facilities offering a range of services aimed at reducing social isolation and providing safe living; these included a disaster volunteer center, a day care center for older adults, a small police station, and a meeting place for each neighborhood association. Each association, comprising some twenty to one hundred households, was relocated to the temporary housing district, keeping its neighborhood so that the district resembled a miniature version of the hometown of Yamakoshi. The most substantial difference between their former hometown and the temporary housing was the availability of a support staff consisting of five people from their thirties to their fifties, including a Buddhist monk and a person with judicial expertise. This staff provided the displaced residents with livelihood support, directed volunteers who came from all over Japan, and arranged a number of entertainment events. These included, for example, a concert of well-known professional singers who were born and raised near the area and a gathering at which the survivors served rice cakes and miso soup to visitors to express their gratitude.

Having lived most of their lives in a relatively remote and quiet mountain area far from the city, the residents associated with the people they met in a quiet and somewhat conservative manner. They seemed, however, to develop new communication skills through socializing with their new neighbors and with outside volunteers. The temporary housing offered crowded and noisy living conditions with little privacy, but the survivors tried their best to deal with the stress and adapt to the situation by incorporating into their daily lives things that represented their hometown and that helped evoke a deeper sense of belonging.

Narratives about Coping with the Stress of Displacement

My interviews revealed that the stress of displacement and of living in temporary housing was ameliorated by at least two tangible things that helped residents maintain a sense of everyday connection with their hometown: wooden statues called Warabe Jizō, a Buddhist saint, which had been carved from a tree that fell during the earthquake, and a vegetable called *kagura nanban*, which the residents grew in the yards around the temporary housing.

Case 1: Wooden Statues

During the interviews, I collected narratives of older adults reminiscing on life in temporary housing such as this one: "The long period of displacement put me under stress, but drinking tea and chatting with the neighbors was of great help. Warabe Jizō was always with us. The statues were very cute, and wore a humorous expression. I felt reassured every time I looked at one and touched it. The scent of Japanese cedar, which was used for the Warabe Jizō statues, also gave me a sense of being home."

The wooden statues with the image of Warabe Jizō were carved from a 180-year-old Japanese cedar that fell in the earthquake. They were carved by a well-known sculptor in Kyoto, who volunteered his time and skills. *Warabe* means "child," and Jizō is a Buddhist saint often represented in statues and, in Japanese folklore, commonly regarded as a children's deity. Jizō legends abound in Japan, where he is believed to be a self-sacrificing savior of those stricken by poverty, illness, disease, and disaster. Generally, Jizō statues are carved from stone, but in this case, the sculptor used a tree that had a direct connection to the hometown of the evacuees. Each statue he carved wears a different humorous facial expression, with a slight smile and a childlike appearance.

Although the residents' attitude toward the statues was influenced by Japanese folklore, the statues also served as memorials dedicated to the memory of the deceased, including animals. After they were transported from Kyoto, the statues were placed in meeting rooms in the temporary housing district. Residents typically used these meeting rooms as tearooms—places to assemble and chat. Although taking tea was an activity originally proposed by the municipal government, the residents made it their own and began to hold tea meetings independently. Some said that in these rooms they sometimes touched the statues' heads with affection, just as they would touch their children or grandchildren. Though the statues had been brought in by outsiders, the survivors embraced them and interpreted them according to their own social context. Interacting with the wooden statues was an important adaptation behavior developed by the displaced residents; it became a way for them to negotiate the unusual living conditions presented by temporary housing.

Six of the eight Warabe statues played this important role in the temporary housing. The remaining two statues were given to other disaster areas: Tokyo's Miyake Island, from which residents were displaced after a volcanic eruption, and Kobe City, which had experienced the Great Hanshin Awaji Earthquake in 1995. Today the six statues have been placed in a corner of Yamakoshi's sightseeing information center, but residents are too busy with work and their daily lives to pay much attention to them. The statues have come to symbolize the recovery of the village from disaster.

Case 2: Vegetable Seeds from Home

To assure their safety, residents were only permitted to visit their hometown once the infrastructure was nearly restored. After that, they began to travel back and forth by car between the temporary housing and their hometown to take care of their homes, farms, and ancestral graves. One narrative, which I paid particular attention to, involved people who brought vegetable seeds to the temporary housing district. They grew vegetables in front of or beside each house, and a new farm was even established near the temporary housing district; it was called the *ikigai* farm, after a Japanese word meaning "human well-being" or "reason to live."

Residents of the town next to the temporary housing district formed a support group for their new neighbors from the mountains, and the displaced residents taught the townspeople to farm vegetables. One of the most popular vegetables, which was new to the town residents, was a hot green pepper called the kagura nanban. Among the displaced residents, the kagura nanban pepper inspired pride and was deeply linked to their identities as residents of the mountains. According to the displaced residents, kagura nanban peppers are insufficiently hot when grown in flatland soil and thus must be grown in rich mountain soil. Furthermore, to ensure that the peppers are sufficiently hot, they believe they must use seeds collected from plants grown in the soil of their hometown; they also believe that the taste of any vegetable grown in mountain soil is better. To me, it seemed that the displaced residents tried to maintain a connection between themselves and their hometown by growing seeds and farm produce such as kagura nanban peppers.[2] This practice illustrates the strong relationship between displaced residents and their hometown, even when they were physically separated from it.

As these two cases demonstrate, people displaced from their homes attempted to maintain a sense of their locality by incorporating into their daily lives things that represented their homes, such as the fallen cedar and the kagura nanban pepper.

Recent Narratives from Older Adults: Family and Hometown

On the surface, the community recovery process appears to have been rapid. However, I met older residents who expressed feelings of unease concerning the speed of recovery and the processes and changes involved in the new development. Disaster recovery does not mean that one's original state is completely restored. For both survivors who chose not to return home and survivors who did choose to return, experiences of loss were often very difficult to accept. At the time of this writing (2017), thirteen years have passed since the earthquake struck, and nine years have passed since the village resumed its administrative functions. A slight change has taken place in the way the older adults narrate their disaster experiences. Whereas earlier interviews focused a great deal on the mutual assistance that was offered during and after displacement, in more recent interviews residents emphasize a strong attachment to their hometown. Recently, I have been hearing more often of older adults who had permanently moved out of the village because they lost their houses in the earthquake but who frequently returned to look after their vegetable gardens. Some older adults regularly came back from their new houses by bus to visit a medical clinic, even though there was a large hospital near their homes in the city. Some former residents continue to maintain their lands and keep their ancestral graves. These may be alternative ways to hold onto a connection with the land after leaving. It is also common for those who decided not to return to reminisce about the good old days they spent in their hometown, even if they now live relatively close.

One day in my fourth year of fieldwork, a woman in her early sixties told me how she felt about her decision not to return to her old home but to move to the new residential district, located about a thirty-minute drive away. She clearly indicated her conflicted feelings: although she liked her new house and neighbors, she missed her old house and neighbors. She often returned to her hometown to see her old friends, to participate in volunteer activities, or to visit welfare facilities to entertain the residents through traditional dance performances. Sharing the time and company of her old neighbors through dancing seemed to be a particularly powerful way for her to feel a physical connection with her hometown.

By contrast, those who decided to return sometimes expressed feelings of emptiness. I once asked an interviewee what she meant when she referred to feelings of emptiness and where she thought they might have arisen from. She said that she could not fully explain where they came from (Taniguchi 2010). But this answer implied that the earthquake greatly influenced her life. It was clear that with regard to where and with whom to live, the feelings of residents varied over time and according to each particular case, and such feelings could change even after decisions had been made.

Whether or not to return to their hometown was largely a family decision. One family told me a noteworthy story. Three generations of the family—grandparents, parents, and children—had lived together. One of the grandchildren was a primary school student, and the family's decision was sparked by a word from this youngest child, who was finding it difficult to adjust to his new school and longing for his old school in his hometown. Two years after the earthquake, the family repaired their house and moved back to restart their lives in their hometown. Some nine years after the disaster, however, they began to sense that each family member felt differently about the decision, because of changes in lifestyle and work environments and divergences in values over time. They said that recently they had each started thinking about what this decision had meant. After all, they could have moved to a place that was more accessible to workplaces and schools; indeed, transportation, especially during the harsh winter, is limited in snowy mountain communities. But despite the clear advantages of living elsewhere, in the end they concluded that they were satisfied with their decision (Taniguchi 2014).

Conclusion

In the first section, I discussed the purpose and research background of this chapter and described how my interviews were accepted by people whose lives had been dislocated by the earthquake. The second section presented a regional outline of the village and the aftermath of the earthquake: I briefly explored the geography, population, and history and detailed the way in which residents were displaced by the earthquake. The third section illustrated two of many means for coping with the stress of life in temporary housing.

Based on narratives collected in interviews, the fourth section examined how older adults of the village attempted to reconnect with their hometown. I discussed how those who chose to leave and those who chose to stay expressed their sense of belonging. Older adults who had lived in the village for many decades before the earthquake had a physical and psychological connection with their hometown.

In my view, those who chose not to return and instead moved to new houses and neighborhoods may have felt that their displacement was ongoing. Thus, they were likely to express stronger, more explicit feelings of connection with their hometown, compared with those who decided to stay (or return). Presumably, one of the ways they reconnected with their hometown after long-term displacement was through the care of their farms and ancestral graves, which evoked their sense of belonging to the place. Except for some new buildings and roads, the rural landscape of the village remains almost identical to the way it was before the earthquake. In part, material objects, such as the statues of Warabe Jizō and the kagura nanban peppers, along with their homesteads, farm, and graves, were meaningful reminders of their hometown.

Similarly, it seemed to me that the farm and the ancestral graves also provided powerful incentives for some older adults to return. One woman in her eighties, now living alone, told me why she decided to return to her hometown by herself, despite the fact that her son tried to persuade her to live with him outside the village. Her decision, she explained, stemmed from the sense of duty and responsibility she felt as a member of a main household with a large and established group of descendants. It was her obligation, she said, to maintain a bond with the other members of the group, and this entailed a responsibility to take care of the house, the farmland, and the family tomb where her ancestors were enshrined. Such "things" helped connect people—physically, emotionally, spiritually—with a time and place before the earthquake and the displacement it caused. These objects allowed them to maintain ties with people and places from the past, even as they worked to reestablish their lives elsewhere.

Catastrophic disasters may destroy the landscape and wash away traces of human activity. When a person's hometown has been destroyed, all the tangible things constituting the landscape and evoking a sense of physical belonging to a home can play a role in mediating the relationship between people and the place (and lives) they left behind. As an ethnographer, I think my way of responding to past and future disasters must be to continue to explore with my interviewees ways to share the stories and the lessons I learned.

Acknowledgments

I would like to thank all of the interviewees. This chapter is based on the following studies and grants: (1) *Chūetsu jishin go no Yamakoshi e no "kison" ni kansuru minzokugakuteki kenkyū* (Grants-in-Aid for Scientific Research (C), research representative: Chin Rei, 2010); (2) "Saigaiji ni okeru kōreisha no shien nettowaaku no kōchiku ni kansuru kōsatsu" (Mitsui Sumitomo Insurance Welfare Foundation, research representative: Taniguchi Yoko,

2007); (3) "Saigai fukkōji no jizokuteki na kōreisha shien ni kansuru chōsa kenkyū" (Taiyo Himawari Kosei Foundation, research representative: Taniguchi Yoko, 2008); (4) "Kakusaka-tagenka suru shōshi kōrei shakai Nihon no kazoku shinzoku kan no sedaisa ni kansuru bunkajinruigaku teki kenkyū" (Grants-in-Aid for Scientific Research, Encouragement of Scientists, research representative: Taniguchi Yoko, 2012).

Notes

1. Some research suggests how older survivors feel when asked to talk about their disaster experiences. Kimura Reo, one of the editors of the *Dictionary of Japanese Disaster History* (Nihon rekishi saigai jiten), has commented on research that shows that survivors older than sixty express the trauma of their disaster experiences and memories more often than younger people do. The research was conducted ten years after the Great Hanshin Awaji Earthquake, which devastated Japan's Kansai region on January 17, 1995 (Kitahara and Kimura 2012, 82–83; Hayashi 2005, 64–49). Respondents were asked whether they thought the following sentences corresponded with their own experiences: (1) I don't want to remember the earthquake; (2) I want to erase all experiences from my memory; (3) I don't want anyone to mention the earthquake; (4) I don't want to hear anything about the earthquake. The results showed that the number of people in their sixties who answered *yes* was almost double that of the other age groups.

Referring to this study, Kimura points out reasons for the differences among the various age groups, suggesting that compared with younger individuals, older adults had less physical strength, vigor, and time to rebuild the areas of their lives that were adversely affected by the earthquake (Kitahara and Kimura 2012, 82–83). Kimura's analysis could lead one to presume that post-disaster trauma is experienced more strongly in villages with aging populations; however, my own studies contradict these findings. Throughout the course of my interviews with older adults, I rarely heard responses such as those listed above. It is not true to say that my interviewees had less traumatic experiences than the older survivors of Hanshin Awaji did, and it should also be borne in mind that the Great Hanshin Awaji Earthquake was of a greater magnitude. To my understanding, however, the scale of a disaster or the structural damage it leaves behind are not the only determining factors of individual mental and physical trauma. Rather, I think that differences in reactions to these events may be deeply related to ways of life, social relationships, environment, and the sense of belonging individuals have had in their daily lives.

2. *Nanban miso*, a handmade flavoring made from hot green kagura nanban peppers and miso, is a popular souvenir of the village.

References

Chin Rei and Niigata kenritsu rekishi hakubutsukan.2010.*Chūetsu jishin go no Yamakoshi e no "kison" ni kansuru minzokugakuteki kenkyū*. Report on Usage of Governmental Research Grant, 2010.

Hayashi Haruo, ed. 2005. *Hanshin Awaji Daishinsai kara no seikatsu fukkō 2005: Seikatsu fukkō chōsa kekka hōkokusho*. Kyoto: Research Center for Disaster Reduction System, Disaster Prevention Research Institute, Kyoto University.

Kitahara Itoko and Kimura Reo. 2012. "Saigaikan no hensen." In *Nihon rekishi saigai jiten*, edited by Kitahara Itoko, Matsuura Ritsuko, and Kimura Reo, 78–83. Tokyo: Yoshikawa Kōbunkan.

Taniguchi Yoko. 2010. "Tsunagu: Saigaifukkōchi ni okeru chiikishakai zukuri no torikumi." In *Kōreisha no uerubiingu to raifudezain no kyōdō*, edited by Suzuki Nanami, Iwasa Mitsuhiro, and Fujiwara Kuniko, 53–67. Tokyo: Ochanomizu Shobō.

———. 2014. "Saigai fukkōchi de saihen sareru 'ko' to kankeisei." In *Shinguru no tsunagu en*, edited by Shiino Wakana, 203–14. Kyoto: Jinbun Shoin.

Ushiyama Motoyuki. 2012. "Shinsai ni tomonau shisha yukuefumei-sha no tokuchō." In *Nihon rekishi saigai jiten*, edited by Kitahara Itoko, Matsuura Ritsuko, and Kimura Reo, 3–6. Tokyo: Yoshikawa Kōbunkan.

Yoko TANIGUCHI is Lecturer of Cultural Anthropology at Meiji Gakuin University and Musashino Art University. She is a contributor to *Gendai kazoku no riaru: Moderu-naki jidai no sentakushi* (Reality of modern family: The options in an era without a model of family; 2021) and *"Hito" ni mukiau minzokugaku* (Folklore facing "people"; 2014).

4

THE STORY OF CULTURAL ASSETS AND THEIR RESCUE

A Firsthand Report from Tohoku

Kōji Katō

IN THE OGATSU-CHŌ DISTRICT OF ISHINOMAKI CITY, a region in Miyagi Prefecture devastated by the Great East Japan Earthquake of 2011, there is an impressive stone monument. It was first erected in 1999 to commemorate the restoration of the district after it was destroyed by another earthquake and tsunami more than half a century earlier. Now, reinstalled after the 2011 catastrophe, the monument stands next to a debris storage site. It speaks poignantly of an endless cycle of destruction and rebirth, and of a land passed from one generation to the next. The inscription reads:

> This district developed long ago as a base for the inkstone industry and the long-distance fishing industry, but on May 24, 1960 much of the current urban area was catastrophically damaged by a tsunami generated by the Chile earthquake.... After overcoming many subsequent difficulties—including the establishment of a ratio for land decrease, provisional designations for land reallocation, acquisition of acreage for parks, the establishment of values of land rights, and the distribution of reallocated property—the elevation of the land for housing and other purposes was raised by approximately two meters and the current urban district was completed. By strange chance, some thirty-seven years from the commencement of construction by my own father, the late mayor Yamashita Matsushiro, I am here as a humble government servant to witness its completion. —Yamashita Toshiro, Mayor of Ogatsu, March 1999[1]

Despite its somewhat technical bureaucratic language, the inscription on the Ogatsu District Land Readjustment Project Completion Monument

Fig. 4.1. Surviving amid the rubble: a stone monument commemorating the restoration of the region after it was destroyed by an earlier earthquake and tsunami. Photograph by author.

tells a story: that the central part of Ogatsu was completely destroyed by a tsunami in 1960, that it took over three decades to restore the area, and that the monument was built in 1999 to commemorate the restoration. What it does not say—but is evident to anybody looking at the monument now—is that twelve years after the joyous unveiling ceremony, the central district of Ogatsu was devastated again, this time by a tsunami approximately fifteen meters high caused by the Great East Japan Earthquake.

To my mind, this monument clearly represents a sense of time unique to an area frequently hit by tsunamis. It took over thirty-five years for residents to reconstruct the city, and the restored town thrived for only a little over a decade before being devastated again. Indeed, the region has been hit by large-scale tsunamis four times in the last 150 years: its history is a narrative of repeated disasters and devastation and of recovery.

The monument also serves as a starting point for contemplating the stories people tell through objects, as well as the stories objects tell about people. As a polished stone slab literally inscribed with words, the monument relates the details of a particular disaster and a particular rebirth. But at the same time, we can also read it within its current context: standing starkly, surrounded by the debris of a more recent disaster, it articulates a broader narrative of death and destruction, of futility and fortitude, of resilience and regeneration. Having emerged on the other side of a new disaster, this monument to destruction and regeneration tells a story that transcends its explicit language and original purpose, imbuing it with new value and new meanings. Bound to a single place but not to a single generation, the monument is a physical item that articulates a complex narrative of past, present, and future.

In this chapter, I discuss a project I have been involved in called a cultural assets rescue operation (*bunkazai resukyū katsudō*), in which we collect materials that have similarly transcended this cycle of disasters and have tales to tell. The materials on which we focus, however, are not objects with explicit commemorative content like a memorial stone; on the contrary, one aim of the current essay is to explore how seemingly unremarkable objects can take on new meanings because of circumstances and tell different stories to different people. Objects rescued from disaster-affected areas may seem at first to be nothing more than evidence of past history and culture, or specimens of natural history. But what deeper meanings do these objects have, and what roles can they play in the future? How do we humans engage with them and make them speak?

In the pages that follow, I briefly discuss a specific project in the Ishinomaki area of Miyagi Prefecture. The project is ongoing and unfolding, and each step of the way takes me into territory I have never explored before; I hope my comments will provide some sense of what it was like to be on the front lines of a rescue operation. What I focus on here is an experience with material items—so-called cultural assets—and the practical aspects of recovering them from the detritus of a disaster that devastated the communities in which they once had a place. In addition to these practical considerations, however, the work we undertook made me reflect more critically and abstractly on the language of "things," the stories that objects tell (or that we tell about objects), and the ways in which human memories and experiences (whether joyous, traumatic, or quotidian) imbue inanimate materials with meaning and values that make them come alive.

Indeed, I hope my comments will contribute to exploring the complex interactions between memories, objects, and narrative, because when we rescue a "thing," we are also continuing a story. With all this in mind, the goals of this essay are to (1) provide a firsthand, on-the-ground account of our rescue activities in one particular place; (2) briefly show how the idea of cultural assets emerges from a longer history of preservation, rescue, and museums; and (3) explore the way cultural assets are part of a complex narrative that is always bound to people, and always changing.

On the Ground: The Cultural Assets Rescue Operation at Ayukawa Repository

The term Great East Japan Earthquake generally refers to all of the damage caused by the magnitude 9 earthquake with an epicenter 130 kilometers east-southeast of the Oshika Peninsula in Miyagi Prefecture that struck on March 11, 2011. This was the largest earthquake ever recorded in this part of Japan. The tsunami it generated, which reached up to forty meters in height in some places, inflicted catastrophic damage on the Pacific coastal areas of the Tohoku and Kanto regions. According to the National Police Agency of Japan, as of March 2021, the death toll was 15,899 and the number of missing was 2,526.[2]

The cultural assets damaged by the Great East Japan Earthquake vary greatly not only in type but also in nature and extent. A number of organizations have been engaged in rescuing damaged assets, including our own Committee for Salvaging Cultural Properties Affected by the 2011 Earthquake off the Pacific Coast of Tohoku and Related Disasters (hereinafter referred to as "Rescue Committee"), the Network for the Preservation of Historical Materials, various public museums, and the editorial offices of local and regional historical publications.[3] The contexts and problems of rescue activities differ from site to site; in fact, this diversity may be one particular feature of the disaster. It will certainly take time to grasp the entire picture, but the first step toward achieving this goal is to share information on efforts being made at each site where rescue has been undertaken. Together with undergraduate and graduate students of Tohoku Gakuin University, located in the city of Sendai, Miyagi Prefecture, I engaged in cultural assets rescue operations at one site. My microlevel report on the activities there should be understood as just a single example of the many diverse rescue operations currently underway.

Tohoku Gakuin University, where I was a faculty member, is responsible for the entire set of disaster-affected materials and documents that were stored in the Ayukawa Repository, a facility under the administration of the Ishinomaki Cultural Center. How did our university, some distance from the Ayukawa area, become the destination for these materials? As far as I remember, I first approached Mr. Kodani Ryūsuke, a prefectural government staff member in charge of rescue operations. I told him that the repository in Ayukawa held a huge collection of disaster-affected cultural assets that should not be dispersed and that we at the university were ready to receive materials and documents and maintain them as a collection. This exchange occurred only one month after the disaster, and we only had limited information, but it was clear that the university could provide great advantages to the cultural assets rescue operation. We had a large number of students who, even without expert skills, could offer human effort and labor; moreover, even though we did not have specialized facilities, we had a space large enough to store the collection, which public museums could not provide. It was thus decided that the Rescue Committee would be responsible for transferring materials and documents from the Ayukawa Repository to Tohoku Gakuin University Museum. At the end of April, we started our preparation for receiving the collection.

The Ayukawa Repository was originally a cultural heritage repository for a town once known as Oshika-chō, which had subsequently merged with Ishinomaki City. Although the facility is called a *repository*, the building itself is nothing more than a prefabricated one-story structure that was used to store a portion of the documents and materials gathered for a book about the history of the town; most of the remaining materials for this historical project were stored in the adjacent Ishinomaki City Oshika Community Center.

The neighborhood of Ayukawa-hama—where these materials came from—is located close to the tip of the Oshika Peninsula. During the Edo period (ca.1600–1868), it was a half-agricultural and half-fishing village, but as the modern whaling industry flourished, it developed into a busy town lined with whaling-related shops and small but vibrant streets for entertainment and shopping. Housing the old Oshika Town Hall, a post office, a bank, and the branch office of the power company, Ayukawa-hama also served as a port for ferries to Kinkasan, a small sacred island venerated by fishing folk. Before the earthquake, the town had a population of approximately 1,200 people.

Closest to the epicenter in a straight line, the Oshika Peninsula was one of the first areas reached by the tsunami. The area has been hit by tsunamis

Fig. 4.2. The central part of Ayukawa region after its destruction by an 8.6-meter-high tsunami. Photograph by author.

four times since the advent of Japan's modern age (the Meiji period, starting in 1868). The tsunami that struck in 2011 reached a height of 8.6 meters; because of the topographic features of the area and the power of the tsunami, the water swept through the town in an instant and ebbed just as fast. The Oshika Branch of Ishinomaki City Hall was opened as an evacuation center, but some people living along the coast of the peninsula evacuated to schools, inns, and private houses that had not been swept away. They had to live together in difficult situations for several months.

The tsunami significantly damaged materials and documents that had been collected for the town-history editing project and for the community center's activities. These materials had been housed in the community center and also in the Ayukawa Repository, both of which were located in the center of town. The community center is a two-story reinforced concrete building; although the first floor was destroyed in the tsunami, the second floor, where the materials were stored, sustained only partial water damage.

At first it was thought that the Ayukawa Repository had been completely lost in the tsunami. However, because of its location behind a strongly built gymnasium, it escaped being swept away. The repository housed archaeological and folkloric materials, fossil remains, and school-related materials and documents from the former Oshika-chō. It had not functioned formally as a museum regularly open to the public, but it was actively used to show how items were stored and also to host educational lectures in which elementary school children could view materials.

The Rescue Committee was able to make its first on-site inspection on June 8, some three months after the tsunami. Removal of debris and the recovery of dead bodies had been undertaken tirelessly since the disaster, and we had been told that some volunteers had already engaged in on-site recovery activities on their own, carrying out initial-phase activities, such as separating debris from the materials scattered throughout the repository. When the committee members visited the affected site, however, we found that the repository had been left unchanged since the tsunami. Broken pieces of what looked like historical items were piled up in a disorderly manner and mixed with debris from houses, abandoned gas cylinders, and many other random objects. A shampoo container hanging from the ceiling indicated that the water had been up to the roof. As the representative of the university, I visited the site along with the director of the community center and experts from a local education board to discuss how to transfer documents. It was obvious at a glance that it would be impossible to store them in the repository itself.

In mid-June, we formed a group consisting mainly of members of the Nara National Cultural Properties Research Institute and the Archaeological Society of Miyagi Prefecture to collect archaeological and geological materials and documents that had survived the disaster. Our rescue activities felt like a kind of excavation. The work done by archaeologists skilled in digging, unearthing, and other groundwork was remarkable, which made me feel strongly that the first people we would need in the field for future rescue operations of damaged cultural assets, whether artifacts or natural history materials, should be archaeologists.

By June 28 and 29, the other members and I were finally able to start collecting folklore materials. Before bringing these items to Tohoku Gakuin University, we first transferred them to the large gymnasium adjacent to the repository; this gym had been used as a morgue immediately after the tsunami, but by this time the dead bodies had been transferred to the morgue

Fig. 4.3. Experts on cultural properties came from all over Japan to participate in the rescue work. Photograph by author.

in Ishinomaki City and a quarter of the gym was left unused. In addition to scholars from the National Museum of Ethnology and the Nara National Cultural Properties Research Institute, we were joined for these two days by researchers from the Niigata Network for Preserving Historical Materials, who had experienced the 2004 Chūetsu-Niigata Earthquake (see chaps. 2 and 3). Experts from various fields and disciplines, ranging from archaeology and ethnology to Western painting, the history of sculptures, literary history, marine biology, and botany worked with us.

It is extremely hot in the Tohoku region in late June, and to make matters worse, it had rained the previous day, so the surrounding area was flooded and the hygienic situation was poor. But our team persevered despite these difficult conditions. Each item brought to the gym for temporary storage was labeled with a rescue number. There were four thousand items in five hundred categories in total, including six hundred boxes of archaeological materials. When rescuing cultural assets, we must follow the same procedures that apply when we borrow an item of cultural property from

Fig. 4.4. The author examining rescued objects brought to the university.

its owner. In our case, the Rescue Committee "borrowed" materials, and we were required to clarify what was contained in each of the numbered bundles or boxes we took out of the repository. Although the final destination of the collected materials was Tohoku Gakuin University in Sendai, there was not enough space to store and handle all the items there at the same time; it was therefore decided that the initial cleaning activity would be performed at the site and that cleaned materials would then be transferred to the university using a four-ton truck approximately once every two weeks. The whole process ended up taking about six months, seven round trips, and ten trucks to complete.

The aim of the initial cleaning procedure was to remove dirt. While I took the lead in providing information on the condition of each item and the best way to clean it, forty undergraduate and graduate students at a time were engaged in cleaning. None of them had any relevant skills or experience, but it was not possible to provide one-on-one instruction. Instead I prepared and provided an information card containing data on the condition of each item and the appropriate procedures to follow. In addition to

Fig. 4.5. *Kamagami-sama*: kitchen guardian-deity figure particular to the Tohoku region. Photograph by author.

students who participated in the rescue operation as part of the practical training program twice a week, a number of students from universities in Tokyo joined us. The process of initial cleaning took an entire year and entailed the assistance of seven hundred individuals.

Concurrent with this cleaning activity, we needed to continually monitor the condition of materials that had already been cleaned. We added all monitoring results to the information cards, including any breakage during cleaning, the recurrence of fungi, and cracks and warping due to dryness. These details, of course, varied by item and by material. For example, historically there is a tradition whereby figures of *Kamagami-sama*, guardian deities of the household, were made by a plasterer with the same clay used to build *tataki* (a hard-packed clay floor) in a house; in recent times, this same deity figure has been constructed of wood. Whether made of clay or wood, a Kamagami-sama is placed for worship on a pillar in the kitchen. Our instructions to clean Kamagami-sama were as follows: because the

Fig. 4.6. University students cleaning folk material items. Photograph by author.

parts made of clay dissolve in water, do not use water; use a brush to remove dirt from the wooden parts; handle the figure carefully when moving it.

Subsequently, we have undertaken secondary cleanings to further improve the condition of materials to a level high enough for them to be displayed and to reduce the risk of deterioration. This process includes monitoring the condition of cleaned items. Further issues and problems we need to address include preventing salt from seeping out of materials that absorbed a large amount of salt during the disaster, and improving the environment of the repository in such a way as to prevent fungus from growing. Not until eighteen months after the disaster was the condition of the collected materials finally stable enough for us to proceed further with their preservation.

Regional Museums, Cultural Assets, and the Making of Meaning

One effect of rescuing and cleaning an object is that its voice becomes singular, released from the cacophony of undifferentiated debris in which it was subsumed. After the initial cleaning process was completed, I began to think more deeply about what it means to care for the things in front of us. It seems to me that the historical and cultural assets of a particular locale should serve as a medium through which people from the present connect with people from the past, and furthermore, such assets should be used as resources for fostering discussion about the future of the region. Preserving such resources should be the primary objective of a cultural assets rescue operation. But what do the assets mean to the people on the ground, whose lives they were a part of?

A nationwide TV program featuring our activities in Ayukawa used such expressions as "cultural assets are regional treasures" and "cultural assets are part of people's identity." Indeed, pithy expressions like these are commonly invoked by government agencies in promoting the protection of cultural assets and museums. These are fine sentiments, of course, but such platitudes do not really reflect the feelings of local residents. It is the government of an affected area, not the residents, that makes a request for cultural assets to be rescued; very few residents care as much about protecting cultural assets as they do about simply preserving their own ability to live. In fact, in Ayukawa most local people were not even aware of the existence of the repository in the first place; it would not have been surprising if, decades from now, the repository's collections had been placed in dead storage or disposed of.

So why, I wonder, does the actual social experience of residents in this community differ so profoundly from the idea of protecting cultural assets? With this in mind, I would like to briefly explore the position of cultural assets affected by the Great East Japan Earthquake in the broader context of the historical development of academic disciplines and museums in this region. I think we can begin by saying that the materials left in the region and affected by the disaster had been maintained by people in the past with the aim of preserving them as a representation of the history and culture of the region. As we undertook our rescue work, we wondered simply why there were so many materials at the site to start with. Why had a municipality as remote as Ayukawa collected so much material and so many documents?

Postwar Research Trajectories

The short answer is, I think, that such collections came as the result of research trajectories that developed in Japan with regard to regional history and folkloristics after World War II, during a period when materials and documents were actively gathered in local areas. One of the major aspects of this trajectory was the construction boom in regional museums that started in the mid-1960s. Museums were built with national subsidies even in remote municipalities; their numbers increased in close association with government policies on tourism, school education, and lifelong learning. Concomitant with this move was a drive to compile volumes on municipal or local history. It usually takes ten to twenty years to complete a local history text like this, and after publication, a large quantity of historical materials and documents remains in the possession of the municipality. Small towns and cities have difficulty organizing these materials and documents; as a result, they are often stored in a room at a library or in a warehouse at the municipal office.

In the case of the former Oshika-chō in Ayukawa, the fact that members of the editorial team had continually worked to organize the materials and documents used for compiling the history significantly facilitated our rescue activities. But this is a rare example. During the postwar development period in Japan, a significant number of excavation surveys were conducted by government agencies, and as a result, municipal governments had to store a large amount of archaeological material. It was left to the discretion of each municipality as to how to deal with these items after completing their reports to the government. Often survey materials gathered at considerable time and cost were simply kept in an increasing number of storage boxes.

From an academic perspective, other reasons for maintaining historical materials in individual regions include the development of regional historical research activities, mainstream research methodologies focusing on regional areas, and region-oriented research approaches premised on the retention of materials at each site. Within the folklore discipline, emphasis was placed on structural-functionalist ethnographic description of various events in self-contained regions with an integrated approach based on nationwide comparative studies. This approach served as a theoretical basis for a movement toward the collection of artifacts from everyday life. Particularly during Japan's high-economic-growth period (ca.1955–73), as lifestyles were changing radically and tools of daily use were being replaced with new ones, people began to feel that they should preserve "old things"—in a sense they conducted their own kind of rescue operation. The governing premise was that the characteristics of a given region could be described and understood by the collecting of material objects. As one aim was to amass a comprehensive number of objects, researchers soon filled up the existing repositories. In more recent years, resident-initiated research activities have focused on community building (*machizukuri*) and environmental conservation; in this context, we can see a nationwide movement in which materials are newly collected and fresh meanings are attached to existing materials.

From a practical perspective, the word *materials* (*shiryō*) is today often replaced with terms such as *regional cultural assets* (*chihō no bunka isan*) or *cultural resources* (*bunka-teki shigen*). Within resident-initiated research activities focusing on community building and environmental conservation, attention has been increasingly directed toward the existence of cultural assets, with regard to both real estate and personal movable properties. Within this context, a large number of cultural assets were affected by the disaster of 2011; because such assets had come to be regarded as essential, local residents felt they had no choice but to take a leading role in regional restoration.

Local Museum History

How does this broader history of museums and attitudes toward cultural assets play out locally in the region from Ishinomaki to the Oshika Peninsula? The oldest museum-like facility in this area is probably the exhibit room of the Miyagi Fishery School, founded in 1897 and now called Miyagi Fishery High School. According to one 1916 source on local history (Takahashi), the Miyagi Fishery School possessed 11 geographical specimens, 66 fishing specimens, 7 fish-farming specimens, and 299 natural history specimens, for a total of 383 items. All these specimens were stored in the exhibition room of the school, where they were used for instructional purposes; during the Taishō period (1912–26), this was one of the very few spaces where people could experience a museum-like way of thinking.

After the Shōwa Sanriku Tsunami of 1933, which caused severe damage to the Oshika Peninsula, we see the advent of a different form of exhibition site: small-scale museum-like structures called *Shinshosai kinenkan* (earthquake and tsunami disaster memorial buildings) built in a number of the affected villages. These museums were constructed to serve not only as exhibition spaces but also as evacuation centers and facilities to help improve the lives of those affected by tsunamis. It is likely they were also used as assembly points and meeting halls. The Shinshosai Museum in Ayukawa was probably constructed at a later date, and according to a book of local history (Oshika-chō shi hensan iinkai 1988), it exhibited whale specimens and other whaling-related materials.

In 1954, at a relatively early point in Japan's postwar redevelopment, another museum was built on the Oshika Peninsula to serve as a municipal whaling resource center, with major exhibitions including whaling tools and specimens of whale parts. In 1990, it was revitalized as Oshika Whale Land, complete with a branch office of the Institute of Cetacean Research. When we conducted our cultural assets rescue operations in 2011, this museum served as one of our largest processing sites.

"Cultural Assets" in the Eyes of Local Residents

Within this broad context of museum construction, activities, and preservation work on a municipal and regional level, I would also like to briefly explore the ways in which present-day residents think about "cultural assets" and objects they hope to preserve and use to represent their existence and lifestyles. One example is a figure of a Buddha missing an arm that was discovered by an employee of a roof-tile company who was volunteering to help remove debris at the main hall of a collapsed temple on the Oshika Peninsula. When I first encountered the object, it was enshrined in a prefabricated, temporary main hall. I was told that the image would intentionally be left unrepaired. From one perspective, of course, an image of Buddha like this is a cultural asset and should be repaired or otherwise maintained in a situation better for its preservation. However, local residents worshipping at the temple chose instead to intentionally keep it unrepaired—that is, in a different sense they had "rescued" a cultural asset.

In contrast, in Ayukawa it was decided very soon after the tsunami that Oshika Whale Land should be restored—a decision that, presumably, reflected the historical and cultural importance of the local whaling industry. Having said that, we should note the comparatively short history of whaling in Ayukawa. During the early modern period, it was limited to the cultivation of beached or stranded whales. Whaling as such did not become a substantial industry until 1906, when Norwegian whaling methods were introduced and full-scale whaling operations began. In other words, Ayukawa is a *modern* whaling town. A number of fishery companies established the port as a base because it was very close to the whaling grounds known as the *Makko* (sperm whale) Castle, due to the large numbers of whales that would gather there. During the early twentieth century, whaling developed into a major industry that included not only plants for processing whale meat and oil but also manufacturers of agricultural fertilizers and gelatin made from whale bones and bone marrow, whale gut strings used for tennis rackets, and other products made from various parts of the whale.

In this way, whaling and peripheral industries were critical for supporting the local economy of the peninsula during and after World War II. But following the International Whaling Commission's commercial whaling moratorium adopted in 1982 and the subsequent ban on commercial whaling implemented in 1988, all whaling ceased. One by-product of the ban was the newly discovered appeal of the whale as a tourism resource; the opening of the renewed Oshika Whale Land in 1990 was both cause and effect of this recognition. The whale was promoted as an iconic resource, with mascot characters of whales appearing throughout the region on billboards and in tourist brochures.[4] While such efforts to harvest the whale as a tourism resource were undertaken, the main targets of the fishing industry itself had shifted to the breeding of coho salmon and Japanese flatfish.

With regard to whales, particular "cultural assets" had long been kept in each whaler's home. When men in Ayukawa sailed across the ocean on whaling ships in the past, they often brought back stuffed specimens of rare birds they had caught or purchased at a port of call. Among these were birds of paradise from New Guinea, Japanese paradise flycatchers from the Philippines, penguins from the Antarctic, and various birds of prey from Australia.[5] Whaling experiences were a source of pride for men in Ayukawa, and these specimens were shown off to guests as proof of this experience and the family's engagement in the industry. Such items rescued from the detritus tell a fascinating story. As "exotic" global treasures, they are poignant markers of a small community's engagement with the world; after the 2011 tsunami, they became all the more meaningful as rescued cultural assets articulating a tale that is both local and global.

Another question that arises is what meaning an item can have when the community to which it belonged no longer exists. This became relevant for a number of everyday articles donated by Dofuku-ji Temple in the neighborhood of Yagawa. In Yagawa, almost every house, every fish-processing facility, and even the elementary school were completely destroyed by the tsunami. After all remaining community property was allocated to the residents, Yagawa itself was disbanded. The Rescue Committee received from Dofuku-ji some thirty folkloric items that had originally been collected by residents who had put together a town history. These materials were the only physical evidence of a community that had lost everything—and essentially ceased to exist. When I discussed this with a man in his forties working on the site, he told me, "The history of our fishing village is over. I want to keep photos and other things to look back on the past, but what are we to do about the cultural assets? They are [only] meaningful to those who live in the area where they belong." In such circumstances, when there are no longer any people living in the neighborhood—when there is no Yagawa community—I wonder what value will be found in the everyday articles we have rescued.

And here is another, similar case. After the earthquake, a lot of the lost personal items that were gathered by volunteers and Self-Defense Forces members were regarded as cultural assets that help maintain memories and ties—such narratives are often featured in TV programs and magazines concerning the tsunami and its aftermath. On the Oshika Peninsula, local residents collected photos, mortuary tablets, graduation diplomas, school uniforms, backpacks, and other personal items from among debris washed ashore. They put them on display at the Oshika Community Center, arranging them by the particular shore where they were found. From an external perspective, we can think of this as a process of redefinition, search and discovery; people who have lost the material base for their living can rely on these items to maintain their memory of life before the tsunami swept through their world.

In reality, however, many of these items have remained unclaimed, and those in charge of the process are worried about how to handle them. Unclaimed items are wide ranging and include such cultural assets as a *shishigashira* (lion-head mask used for ritual performance). The shishigashira that washed ashore is a kind used during Haru Kito (spring prayers), a popular seasonal event performed on many parts of the peninsula. Even a year after this particular shishigashira was found on the beach, no one had come to claim it. In a sense, because it is not associated with a particular place or community or people who feel attached to it, this was a cultural asset whose meaning had yet to be discovered. It was a cypher, a symbolic object detached from its narrative context. Eventually it came to light that the shishigashira belonged to a village in the vicinity of Onagawa. Only after it was finally identified with a particular place and group of people— and it was decided that an event would be organized for its return—did the shishigashira take on meaning and assume a new role in the story.

Indeed, in many ways the process of rescue is one of giving meaning to objects, of identifying their place in a wider narrative. Like the narration of a story, it is a process of choosing and editing and distinguishing. Even an activity as seemingly mundane as debris removal entails the separation of useful things from unnecessary things; in our own rescue operation, things that were considered useful—in other words, things regarded as *cultural assets*—were rescued and cleaned. This critical act of separation also seems to apply to the sorting of things within individual houses. For example, people cannot bear to dispose of household altars and shrines or figurines of gods, such as the seven deities of good fortune, but at the same time they do not know what to do with them when there is no space to store them. Instead of disposing of them as debris, they often offer them to shrines. In Watanoha in Ishinomaki, for instance, people have brought household altars, miniature shrines for Omyojin-sama (household god of Inari), and wooden statues of Daikoku and Hotei to a shrine. And at the shrine they have also organized a project to gather votive tablets (*ema*), each with an inked handprint of a child on it that had been offered on the occasion of the celebration of a child's third, fifth, and seventh birthdays. Household sacred items as well as votive tablets are objects that have been literally dis*placed* by the tsunami; having lost their homes, as it were, they can only be properly kept in the sacred space of a shrine.

Symbols and Monuments

In one of the programs developed to support people affected by the disaster, activists and artists from outside the region were invited to build installations together with local residents. To produce objects under the theme of memories, they selected symbolic items from the debris and displayed them according to the messages they wanted to articulate, such as healing, remembrance, repose, solidarity, perseverance, life, and nature worship. Within the context of this expressive project, nonprofit organizations and artist groups organized and implemented exhibitions at elementary schools and senior high schools.

Also, in the media, photographers have published images of landscapes with compositions that seem beyond human comprehension: a ship and bus on top of a building, bicycles piled up, a single surviving pine tree, a collapsed building, a ruined elementary school. I thought I was fed up with this kind of symbolic expression of the trauma of the disaster, but now when I take a second look at photos like these I find that I also feel a connection to such symbolic landscapes. We who survive in the present unconsciously tend to use specific objects or landscapes as unifying symbols to represent the diverse aspects of a massive disaster; these images and objects are symbolically powerful because they defy human comprehension and our conventional understandings of the natural order of things, and thus, they powerfully articulate otherwise inexpressible emotions.

Similarly, after the tsunami certain large items of debris on the landscape became monumentalized simply because they were difficult to remove and, as a result, were seen by many people. Such striking and constantly viewed landmarks acquire a powerful symbolic value. In Ishinomaki, for example, a huge tank shaped like a can of Yamatoni canned whale meat, which had stood as a distinctive advertisement for many years, was severely damaged by the tsunami and lay on its side, dented and rusting. On one end of the can, somebody had spray-painted a picture of a floating bottle with the words "we are all one." The tank became an important landmark visited and photographed by volunteers from outside the affected area. It was transformed into a monument to the community and the disaster. When it was finally removed in 2012, many people opposed its erasure from the landscape.[6]

Indeed, the concept of cultural assets is premised on the possibility of *representational* activity. Things that were intended to be consumed or discarded end up being preserved in order to represent certain historical trends or critical moments of transformation. The very act of placing an item in a museum can be thought of as a kind of rescue activity that creates meaning, and representational value, in the moment. But who and what has the capacity to give an object meaning and value? Can we say that an object rescued by a specialist is a cultural asset but that an item rescued by a nonspecialist is merely based on fetishism? I cannot stop dwelling on such questions. Indeed, ever since my experiences in Ayukawa, I have come to understand that visually, just by looking, it is impossible to separate "cultural assets" from debris.

Listening to the Stories Cultural Assets Can Tell

Disaster changes the stories an object tells. From my observations, for example, I realized that it is difficult to avoid treating disaster-affected cultural assets as monuments—especially when, like the giant can of whale meat, they are displaced and shifted onto a defamiliarized landscape. On the other hand, even if we return rescued collections to the places they were before the disaster, it is not always possible to endow them with new value. It was my conviction, however, that there must be a way to discover new meanings for objects through the process of rescue itself—and this is what I undertook as I worked with students. With this in mind now, I return to our own rescue project and our attempt to understand the stories objects can tell.

As mentioned, most of the items originally housed in the Ayukawa Repository had been collected as folkloric materials that demonstrated how life on the Oshika Peninsula was lived in the past. Such items of material folklore are valuable because we have what I call back data—that is, information about how they were produced and used in everyday life. However, if we have no back data for an item damaged by the tsunami, it becomes indistinguishable from the other debris. With this in mind, students of the folklore seminar of Tohoku Gakuin University who had been engaged in the cleaning process visited the affected site in August 2012 and began organizing outreach activities to display disaster-affected materials on the first floor of Oshika Community Center in Ishinomaki City. Our assumption for this project was that with rescued materials displayed in front of them, those individuals who had experienced the disaster would be inspired to speak—we would be able to hear their stories and also learn the background data associated with the objects themselves. And indeed they did speak, with passion, about the relationship between their own experiences and the materials at hand, relating sentimental memories of these tools and objects, explaining how they were used, and even taking them up in their hands.

First, a little more background on the project itself: the exhibition was mainly coordinated by about twenty juniors from the folklore seminar of the Department of History, Faculty of Letters, of Tohoku Gakuin University. During the first half of 2012, in our practical training class on folklore, we prepared the exhibition in conjunction with the preservation of materials. We transferred approximately one hundred items to the exhibition site, a number that accounted for no more than 3 percent of all the folkloric materials we were temporarily retaining at the university. We felt this relatively small number of items was appropriate for what was really a test case of interviewing local people to gather information. (Moreover, we only had a single large van at our disposal, and therefore it was not possible for us to carry more than one hundred items.)

Folklore materials must be packaged and treated appropriately before they are transferred, which requires special skills and the expertise of curators. Even though the cultural assets to be transferred were disaster affected and broken or in disrepair, this was a perfect opportunity for students to acquire technical skills as curators. We decided to hold the exhibition in the former community center even though the building, which had been hit directly by the tsunami, was to be demolished in December 2012 because of possible structural damage. We dared to use this building not because we wanted to show the structure itself as a monument but simply because so much of Ayukawa had been swept away by the tsunami that there was no other place for people to gather. The building had already been used as a base for volunteers from outside the affected area until June. (During the eighteen months after the disaster, more than forty-five thousand volunteers visited Ayukawa.) Several temporary shops, a bank, and some housing units had been established nearby, and local residents regularly used the community center's parking lot. In short, the community center was one of very few public places where a range of people—including local residents, employees of companies engaged in restoration construction, and volunteers—would regularly come together.

Timing was also important. In Japan, we have an annual summer holiday called Obon, during which people living away from their hometowns return to gather with family members to remember their ancestors. Although people would be busy welcoming visitors, preparing special meals, and participating in temple events, we thought they might be willing to take some time to come visit the exhibition, so we decided to hold the exhibition for three days from August 12 through 14. (The Obon holiday in this region is celebrated from August 13 through 15.)

On August 11, the students and I loaded materials into the van and headed to Ayukawa, arriving at the community center around noon. After finishing lunch at a temporary eating establishment, we set to work cleaning and setting up the center. For security reasons and because no electricity was available, we had to complete all work by sunset; we worked quickly and managed to set everything up in three hours.

On the first day of the exhibition, there were very few visitors at the beginning. While the media was interviewing us, however, local people gradually started to gather at the site, and the students set to work. First, they asked visitors basic questions, such as their address before the earthquake, current address, age, name, and reason for visiting the exhibition. Through this sort of straightforward conversation, many of the local people became interested in the work with which the students were engaged, and the interviews became more serious for the purposes of our project; students asked visitors to talk about memories and anecdotes associated with the displayed materials. Some interviewees discussed their experiences in the past, and others, their current daily lives. Some talked about how terrible it was when the disaster occurred and about the efforts they had made since.

The exhibit included daily necessities such as clothing, food and personal items, agricultural and fishing tools, and charms used by people to pray for the welfare of their family and for a good harvest or a good catch. While looking at these items of everyday life from about fifty to a hundred years ago, visitors seemed to be flooded with memories of all sorts, many from before the disaster. When we planned the interviews, we had expected that people would discuss their experiences with the earthquake and tsunami. But they mostly talked about their memories of the good old days and ways to use the tools they saw. Many of them would actually pick up an item on display and passionately speak of their experience with it.

In a sense, therefore, the narratives inspired by these items were not stories of disaster and loss but rather accounts of the routines of daily life in an earlier time. Indeed, even though volunteers and government agency staff talked about the earthquake and the tsunami, very few local residents actually focused on these subjects. And although the media seemed to be interested in recording memories of the disaster itself, in reality the information gathered from the residents was rather similar to data usually obtained through regular folklore surveys.

Having said this, however, there is ultimately a qualitative difference between data from the usual folklore surveys and the comments offered by people who had experienced material losses in the disaster. One middle-aged woman, for example, explained that because she had lost the physical objects that were the sources of her memories, she had not talked about the past since the disaster. In a sense, then, the tools and other items rescued by researchers helped visitors look back to a time before the losses incurred in the tsunami; through the rescued materials, people were able to remember their pasts again. We might say that the display served as a cognitive bridge across the moment of disaster, allowing residents to

Fig. 4.7. At a facility for seniors, university students conduct an interview on the history of everyday life on Oshika Peninsula. Photograph by author.

recall a time when such objects were still present in their lives—when these "cultural assets" displayed in a museum-like setting were simply the tools of everyday life. To be sure, visitors to the exhibition may have initially felt somewhat uncomfortable being interviewed by our students, but what made the greatest impression on me was the look of contentment they had when they left.

During the three days of the exhibit, we completed about 180 interview sheets. Approximately two-thirds were from local residents, and the others were mostly from volunteers who came from outside Ayukawa. And we are continuing and expanding this sort of exhibition and interview process. What do people talk about when they see these rescued materials? What narratives do these objects inspire? As we continue to collect information, we discover that it may contain not only an explanation of a tool or technique but also a comparison of life in the past and present and a discussion of the way things have changed in the region—all data that, I think, is different in nature from the sort of information obtained from conventional folklore surveys. In fact, it is our objective as we move forward not to be confined to standard survey methods, which are based on the assumption that only those people who are originally from the region can identify the meaning of material found there. We want to go beyond the belief that only narratives told by ordinary, nameless people can define the meaning of a material object. Why shouldn't we take into account all manner of narratives, including explanations by specialists, stories of experiences directly told by local residents, strategic narratives based on the intentions of a local person of importance, and even stereotypical characterizations promulgated by the media? All of these should be considered data accompanying the presence of a collection. By accumulating a network of narratives like this, we hope we can leave a fuller record of these objects—and of the varied ways of life in which they played a part—for generations to come. We held such exhibitions thirteen times from 2012 to 2016 and completed thousands of interview sheets.

The Life Story of Things

The disaster-affected cultural assets that are temporarily stored in Tohoku Gakuin University Museum are one set of materials from the Ayukawa Repository, which itself emerged as part of the development process of the history of museums and the history of folklore research since before World War II. It was used effectively in activities by community centers and for school education; the objects held there were maintained, without being disposed of, because of the faith of local intellectuals, including the editorial members of the town history, local historians, and the director of the community center. Then they were destroyed by the tsunami on March 11, left untouched for three months, rescued by teams from around the nation, and cleaned by university students. Through this complex and ongoing process, involving many people from many places, our cultural assets rescue operation shifts from activities of physical conservation to activities in which new meanings are created.

Every object, every thing, has a story to tell. Some are explicit and purposeful, like the monument stone with which I began this essay—literally inscribed with words, made all the more meaningful by its current location. Other objects are quieter and have to be coaxed into telling their tales. But these stories are the ones that are so important to rescue, not just because

Fig. 4.8. "Celebration of the whale festival": a flyer for the
twelfth Cultural Assets Rescue Exhibition, held in
August 2016.

they are memories of a lost past but because they create meaning for people
living in the present, and in the future.

Afterword, Added in 2021

In the ten years since the Great East Japan Earthquake, we have held
twenty-five exhibitions. In each, disaster survivors played a leading role
in determining and narrating exhibit content. The older residents of the
Tohoku region selected many of the exhibited objects and narrated their
history and uses; younger student survivors recorded and helped present the stories created from the interplay of words and objects. In 2019,
I moved from Tohoku Gakuin University to Musashino Art University.

Currently, I am working with art students to find a new approach to representing the local culture of the disaster area through art and design. Before the tenth anniversary of the catastrophe, a national park visitor center and a museum of whale culture opened in Ayukawa Port. That exhibit was planned using data from our interviews and ethnographic research. A brief account of our post-tsunami exhibition techniques will appear in English in a forthcoming volume to be published by Japan's National Museum of Ethnology.

Notes

* This article is partially based on a previous essay written by the author in Japanese (Katō 2012). The current version has been significantly revised and rewritten by the author with major translation, editorial, and writing assistance from Michael Dylan Foster. Please note, although the essay itself has been updated, we have retained the author's vision (and the details he presents) of the activities in the several years immediately following the earthquake and tsunami; thus, the essay provides a rare snapshot from the midst of the recovery activities.

1. The Chile Earthquake of 1960 occurred on May 22, 1960. With a magnitude of 9.5, it is considered the largest earthquake of the twentieth century. The temblor and tsunami that followed left approximately 1,655 people dead in Chile, Hawaii, the Philippines, and Japan. In Japan, a 5.5-meter-high tsunami struck the coast of Honshu the day after the quake itself; 185 people were reported killed or missing, and there was approximately $50 million in damage. See "USGS M 9.5—1960 Great Chilean Earthquake (Valdivia Earthquake)," updated November 7, 2016, https://earthquake.usgs.gov/earthquakes/eventpage/official19600522191120_30 /executive.

2. See National Police Agency, "Police Countermeasures and Damage Situation associated with 2011 Tohoku district—off the Pacific Ocean Earthquake," accessed March 26, 2022, https://www.npa.go.jp/news/other/earthquake2011/pdf/higaijokyo_e.pdf.

3. For the Rescue Committee, see http://www.tobunken.go.jp/english/rescue/index.html; for the Network for the Preservation of Historical Materials, see http://siryo-net.jp/.

4. These efforts continued after the earthquake, as women in Ayukawa resumed making braided *misanga* friendship bracelets from fishing nets and residents printed whale images on seals and T-shirts to attract attention to the restoration.

5. It is said that some people accidentally caught penguins in the Antarctic and froze them along with whales to bring back to Japan, where they were stuffed.

6. For more on this tank, including photographs of its removal, see *Nikkei shinbun* (2012).

References

Katō Kōji. 2012. "Tohoku gakuin daigaku ni okeru hisai bunkazai e no shien katsudō." In *Kioku o tsunagu: Tsunami higai to bunka-isan*, edited by Hidaka Shingo, 68–86. Osaka: Senri bunka zaidan.

Nikkei shinbun. 2012. "Ishinomaki no 'kyodai kanzumei' kaitai." June 30, 2012. http://www
.nikkei.com/article/DGXZZO43226870Q2A630C1000000/.
Oshika-chō shi hensan iinkai eds. 1988. *Oshika-chō shi.* Oshika-chō: Oshika-chō shi hensan
iinkai.
Takahashi Tetsugyū. 1916. *Oshika-gun annai-shi.* Rikuyōsha shuppanbu.

Kōji KATŌ is Professor of Japanese Folklore Studies and Museology at Musashino Art University. He is author of *Tsunami to kujira to pengin to*
(Tsunami, whale, and penguin; 2021).

5

CRITICAL EMPATHY
A Survivor's Study of Disaster

Kate Parker Horigan

A S A RESIDENT OF NEW ORLEANS FROM 2001 to 2008, I lived through and closely observed Katrina's impact. My cultural background, race, and socioeconomic status influenced my decision and ability to evacuate safely, to live elsewhere for three months, and to return. Nonetheless, the depression, disruption, loss, and frustration that accompanied my experience have profoundly shaped the way I understand the experiences of others. My role as a survivor informs my research with personal narratives of other survivors and suggests general principles about the role of survivor-ethnographers in a ground-up approach to studying and responding to disaster. Though this position can be conflicted in many ways, pitting emotional experience and objective observation against each other and providing insight by way of privilege, it also enables a productive stance of critical empathy—of understanding with a difference.

Role Conflict: Becoming a Survivor-Ethnographer

Hurricane Katrina was the first time—thanks to my relative privilege—that I experienced displacement from and destruction of my home. For years afterward, I was afraid to leave home for any extended time, and when I did, I felt a constant nagging anxiety. There was also the anxiety of living in post-storm New Orleans, where suicide rates rose, fires raged, armed troops roamed, and ordinary activities such as driving were inordinately stressful: there were broken streetlights, National Guard tanks, and visible reminders of devastation everywhere. My roommate ended up in the hospital after accidentally inhaling mold from a piece of salvaged furniture. Our environment was literally toxic.

Katrina, though, also shaped the path of my career. I was working on a master's degree in English when the storm hit, and my focus on literature shifted to a focus on oral narratives, specifically those describing traumatic experiences of the hurricane. This seemed many things at the time—random, unavoidable, fortuitous—but only in retrospect does it appear to me as a pattern in scholarship on disaster. I am not alone in having focused my academic energies on a catastrophic event that unexpectedly hit home, and this pattern merits serious consideration. Scholars have a potentially privileged relationship to disaster, and keeping a critical lens on that relationship is necessary to keep our work from exploiting other survivors. It is my hope, though, that the local knowledge and personal perspective of survivor-scholars can illuminate the expertise of other locals, which is too often ignored in recovery efforts.

Those who find themselves thrust into the simultaneous position of survivor and scholar face obstacles in reconciling these roles. As Kristen Barber (2007, 87) puts it, "it is difficult to do hurricane victim and academic at the same time." In a handful of articles and collections devoted to this topic in the wake of Katrina, social scientists explore these conflicting demands. Haney and Barber (2013) explain that survivor-scholars are faced with balancing academic expectations of objectivity against their subjectively reached understanding of disaster. They connect this tension to larger theoretical claims about the value of personal experience in scholarship: "The subjectivity so inherent to experiences of strife is left out of our sociological understandings of disaster, and so we miss out on what many feminists and scholars of color see as an integral aspect of seeing the world: experience" (110). As evidence of this trend after Katrina in particular, they point to the disproportionate amount of social scientific research conducted by outsiders (107).

Barber (2007, 81) references Goffman's notion of "role conflict" in describing the incompatible positions of emotional survivor and unemotional scholar and writes that after Katrina she was "forced to . . . make salient my role . . . as a productive 'masculine' academic." I experienced this role conflict as well, as a graduate student displaced in the wake of Katrina. When the hurricane caused Tulane University to close for the fall of 2005, I temporarily enrolled at Columbia University to continue my graduate work there. Though the administrators and professors were generous in admitting me into small graduate seminars, other students told me that I was taking up space for which their more qualified peers had competed. I was not offered consolation or support, despite my precarious emotional state. As a result, I felt the need to distance myself from my role as a suffering survivor and prove my ability to fulfill the role of worthy (unemotional, productive) academic. To be sure, encountering a cold reception at a prestigious graduate institution is a privileged form of exclusion. But I share this account and ones like it because they illustrate a larger pattern of conflicting roles for survivor-scholars.

Conflicting demands continue to characterize my experiences with sharing knowledge about Katrina, whether on the page or in the classroom. Years after my evacuation and semester in New York, following my return to and graduation from Tulane, I was pursuing a PhD at Ohio State, writing a dissertation about Katrina narratives, and teaching undergraduate English and folklore classes. In one of my classes, I showed the documentary *Trouble the Water*, which features an African American couple from New Orleans's Ninth Ward who survive the flooding of their neighborhood (Deal and Lessen 2008). Kim Roberts shares her firsthand footage of the storm, and the film follows Kim and her husband, Scott, through the trials of rebuilding. I presented the film to students as an example of unique documentary style (incorporating a subject's own footage), but in an effort to appear neutral and present an academic rather than emotional perspective, I did not contextualize the film as emotionally disturbing. In part to conceal my own emotional response to the film, I watched with my back to the class, and I only realized after turning around at the end that a student was distraught and in tears. As it turned out, the young woman had family in Louisiana and had been reminded of their traumatic experiences and her own fear for their lives during that time. She was one of only a few African American students in the class. I felt I had done all of them but especially her a disservice by not attending to the emotional aspects of the film—both to prepare them and to better contextualize her response for the other, slightly baffled, white midwestern students. By devaluing my own emotional response to Katrina, I had seemingly devalued hers as well. Situations like that one drive me to further recognize and perhaps even reconcile the conflicting roles of survivor and scholar, in order to do justice to both.

"Out of Sorrow": Folklorists as Survivor-Ethnographers

Although the roles of survivor-scholars complicate academic lives and work, it is encouraging that in the discipline of folklore, in recent decades at least, reflexivity on the part of the researcher is accepted and, to some extent, expected (Lawless 1992; Borland 1998). We recognize that in ethnography our primary tool for research is our own human self and that since such an instrument does not allow for impartial observation, our best hope is to own up to our partialities. We have applied this reflexivity to our relationships with collaborators; to our positions of power; and to our identities, including gender, race, class, religion, ability, and sexual orientation. We need to more fully explore, however, the standpoint of "survivor" as it relates to ethnographic research and applications of folklore.

In the wake of September 11, folklorists including Kay Turner and Steve Zeitlin were called to action in New York. Turner (2009, 156) describes her experience of watching the Twin Towers fall and seeing "so much gone, so quickly, in the blink of my eyes." She writes, "Out of sorrow, out of a need I could hardly articulate, I, like so many others, was drawn to Union Square numerous times in the first days after the attacks" (162). Turner positions herself clearly as a grieving survivor. Yet it is through her participation in this ritual of grief—going to Union Square and observing the spontaneous memorials there—that she begins to build her scholarly conclusions. She notes the ephemeral nature of vernacular responses to the tragedy and suggests that though "folklorists tend to stand by tradition . . . the ephemeral is also necessarily within our purview" (159). She writes especially poignantly of the sensory experiences of being a survivor in New York: "Certain of the ephemeralities of September 11th, such as odor, are fixed particularly and indelibly in somatic memory . . . composing a catalog of potent evidence in the bodily archive of those who were here that day" (179). The objective scholar may be curious about sensory experiences and memories of disaster, but only the subjective survivor can truly access them. In a similar vein, Haney and Barber (2013, 113) write, "Our non-academic selves experience the uncertainty of evacuation and displacement, the smell of mold and rot, and the inundation of our city." Though they present these experiences as burdens for social scientists, they are also a boon: for example, folklorists who are on the scene can illuminate the embodied experiences so critical to understanding disaster. Perhaps more significantly, they can make the case for such specialized knowledge of other survivors, sparking a public realization that survivors are the best sources of knowledge about what is happening in their communities and how it can be addressed.

Beyond the disciplinary leaning toward reflexivity, folklorists possess ethnographic, documentary, and archival skills that prove useful in contexts of disaster. As a result, folklorists can find themselves in the position of cultural first responders, called on to interpret the wreckage and tend to the rent social fabric of communities. Like Turner, in 2001 Steve Zeitlin found himself unexpectedly in a disaster-stricken city. He describes the joint roles he and his coworkers occupied as "participants in grief, New Yorkers as well as folklorists" (2006, 102). He quickly recognized that their professional expertise was in demand: "By the time the staff of City Lore were able to get back into our downtown East Village office a few days later, we already had email messages asking us to document the spontaneous memorials and collect stories. . . . The decision was made before we had time to think about it" (102). Other folklorists describe similar moments when personal suffering and career paths unexpectedly collided. Sylvia Grider (2001), for instance, began studying vernacular responses to sudden death after a tragic incident on her campus. She writes that her work in this area stems from "personal experience as Principal Investigator of the Bonfire Memorabilia Collection Project at Texas A&M University, which I organized and directed following the collapse of the student bonfire in November, 1999, which killed twelve of our students" (1).

When Madrid was rocked by a massive deadly attack on commuter trains in 2004, folklorist Cristina Sánchez-Carretero was thrust into the role of survivor-ethnographer. She remembers: "After the bombings, a group of anthropologists and literature scholars at the Spanish National Research Council (CSIC), and members of a CSIC research group on expressive culture in contemporary societies started a project to document and analyze the public expressions of grief. . . . In a sense, our going to the stations with our cameras constituted an academic way to process our own grief" (2011, 246). Like Turner, Zeitlin, and Grider, Sánchez-Carretero applied the skills of her academic discipline to the situation at hand. Like the others as well, she recognized the inextricable relationship of her emotions to this work. In fact, Sánchez-Carretero expands on this, noting that "Grief (and other emotions) is an effective trigger mechanism for actions of various kinds, including the actual academic endeavor, constituting what can be called an 'emergency ethnology'" (246). Not only are we called to action by others; we are driven to it by the need to respond and assuage our own feelings of helplessness. An "emergency ethnology" is one employing "rapid-response strategies that will enable professionals in ethnology to actively transfer the type of knowledge we produce to society" (Sánchez-Carretero and Ortiz 2008, 26).

This sort of emergency scholarship, participated in and noted by other folklorists, requires more attention than we have given it to date. My focus, though, is less on the skills that we can apply and more on the essential fact of our expertise as survivors, as well as our position as professionals who value the knowledge of locals and community insiders. Rather than posing an obstacle to our work, this duality ought to help us better serve disaster-affected communities. Particularly, survivor-ethnographers are in a good position to spotlight the expertise of other survivors who occupy less visible platforms. As one case in point, I have focused my research on the circulation of Katrina survivors' personal narratives, after my own experience brought to light a larger pattern of survivors' rhetorical exclusion and displacement in public discourse.

Rhetorical Displacement Post-Katrina

Narratives about Katrina that typically reach large audiences are those that uphold dominant narratives and reinforce popular beliefs. My recognition that published accounts of the hurricane were oversimplified was fostered in part by the feelings of exclusion I experienced when I heard them. Once I realized that many widely circulated versions of personal suffering were perpetuating stereotypical representations of survivors, I began a process of research informed by community experts. I did this primarily through my involvement with the oral history project Surviving Katrina and Rita in Houston (SKRH), wherein survivors interviewed other survivors, producing narratives that document their experiences as shared on their own terms.[1] Listening to interviews from SKRH, I studied the conditions that enabled those remarkable stories to emerge. Then I compared those conditions to the more common ones in which Katrina stories are shared publicly—through books, movies, and other popular media. I discovered that survivor-to-survivor interviews are characterized by negotiations of context, essentially guidance for the listener on how to hear the story. That negotiation is missing in published versions of personal narratives; as a result, survivors appear to be represented in true-to-life ways but in fact are reduced to stereotypes, with all of their input on their portrayal ultimately silenced in the process of publication. My study represents one way to learn from the expertise of survivors: if we can model the circulation of personal narratives after the storytelling context that survivors create for themselves, then we can promote a more ethical means of sharing stories of disaster.

My own experiences of misrepresentation were partly what led me to listen to survivor interviews and to recognize survivors' implicit and explicit concerns about how they are portrayed. For me, and for so many others in more extreme ways, our displacements were multiple and complex. There was the obvious physical, geographical displacement. But the less obvious aspect is rhetorical displacement, or exclusion from the dominant discourse about our shared experiences and our home. This second displacement manifested on both small and large scales, with variable consequences. For example, like many of the SKRH interviewees, I did not recognize my story among those stories broadcast on the news. The media coverage obscured the diversity of experience, electing instead to show masses of undifferentiated suffering bodies. The result was to depict primarily the city's working-class African American population and to frame them as either destitute and helpless or irresponsible and violent. The video loops and still photographs that news organizations chose to highlight bolstered this depiction. These showed either individual faces with anonymous and abstracted sorrow or large groups of angry people. In this way, media coverage was read in terms of (and perpetuated) national stereotypes about African American poverty. Showing only helpless or angry people of color reinforced dominant, racist misperceptions that New Orleans's African American population comprised solely passive victims and dangerous criminals. The verbal counterpart to these images is found in those stories whose accelerated circulation reveals their discursive power. For example, the rumors that Carl Lindahl (2012) identifies as characterizing African American survivors as a threat to potential first responders were quickly and uncritically instituted as official knowledge. In short, the visual and verbal rhetoric that defined Katrina in popular discourse left no space for the diverse experiences and identities that actually make up the event and the city.

In my case, as a middle-class, white transplant from the East Coast, the absence of my story in news coverage did not equate to devastating consequences as it did for others. Not being noticed is far less harmful than being labeled as unworthy of help or as a threat to helpers. For instance, no law enforcement officers tried to stop me as I evacuated from New Orleans in the middle of the night. I was, though, questioned by National Guard soldiers when I returned weeks later to see what I could salvage from the house I had been renting. Their Humvee pulled up as I carried a box of water-warped books down my front steps. They were forceful and frightening, and they did not leave until I produced a lease with my name and a matching driver's license, proving that I had a right to take my ruined things from the house where I used to live. However, in stark contrast to the treatment an unthinkable number of New Orleanians endured, those men with guns asked for identification before arresting—or shooting—me, and they believed me when I claimed my innocence. This ironically was thanks in part to the one-dimensional representation of Katrina's survivors: faces that looked like mine had not been featured on the nightly news and had not been linked to pernicious narratives about looting and other criminal behavior.

My invisibility in the representations of Katrina did not preclude, as the wrong kind of visibility did for others, my ability to find material, financial, and emotional assistance. The resources I was able to draw on—namely family and friends who lived outside the bounds of New Orleans and who had the means to help me—were not available to a huge proportion of those most affected. Even the resources I was able to rely on, though, were stretched thin. The costs quickly multiplied: gas, hotel stays, plane tickets, restaurant meals, not to mention new clothes when the three-day supply I had packed was exhausted. The time was longer than anyone anticipated, and houseguests generally have an expiration date. When my car, left in New Orleans, was declared a total loss, I could not replace it. When the Federal Emergency Management Agency (FEMA) sent me a check, an automatic "disaster assistance payment" of $2,000, it went quickly to cover the expenses of suddenly relocating and starting from scratch. When several months later FEMA requested that I pay them back, citing insufficient evidence that I had lived at my flooded address, I could not afford to return the money to them. I endured months of maddening conversations with and threats from that agency until they finally, inexplicably, retracted their request. Nevertheless, I always had a level of security, a safety net, which even that official attempt at erasing my experience did not fully destroy. I describe my own exclusion from Katrina's dominant narratives here to illustrate how even for someone with a comparatively strong system of support, the effects of rhetorical displacement are immediate, immense, and lasting. Understanding this has driven me to study, and ultimately attempt to redress, this exclusion on a larger scale, especially when it has consequences that I have not had to endure.

"Little Refugee": Unpacking Privilege and Applying Insights

Although my displacement provided me with special insight, it does not nullify the privilege that protected me throughout Katrina. Insight and privilege go along with the conflicting roles of survivor and academic, and this complex relationship deserves attention. On the one hand, it has been tempting for me to disregard or minimize the insights I have garnered because I do not feel comfortable claiming the status of survivor or speaking on behalf of or with those whose lives were lost or more drastically reconfigured than my own. On the other hand, privilege has afforded me a position from which to observe, speak, and advocate for those who do not have the same access to resources that I have. Referring to social scientists who reflect on their experiences as survivor-scholars, Danielle Hidalgo (2007, 4) writes, "Many of us are located in positions of relative privilege. However, we believe it is important to reflect on the workings of privilege, as well as disadvantage, in order to better understand how inequality shaped options, choices, and experiences of Hurricane Katrina." In the spirit of such reflection, I offer one piece of my Katrina story that I am generally reluctant to discuss in academic contexts, partly because it highlights personal emotion and partly because it is a story in which I fear others will locate my privilege and discredit my insights.

I initially evacuated to a friend's home in Nashville, where we spent days sleeping on the floor, obsessively calling disconnected numbers, searching images of Google Earth, and binge-watching CNN. It became clear that I would not be able to return to New Orleans as expected. I asked my parents for help in purchasing a plane ticket, and I boarded a flight to their home in Maryland. I was numb, exhausted, and unsure what would happen next. I had no way of finding out the extent of flooding in my neighborhood or the status of my residence and belongings. I had friends in New Orleans who I had not yet heard from, and I did not know whether I would ever hear from them again. I had been left raw by the horrific images of my fellow New Orleanians waiting and dying in the streets of our city. When I got off the plane and saw my father, though, I felt a surge of relief so intense that I wept. As he hugged me, he smiled and said, "Oh, my little refugee!" It was a term of endearment, a comforting welcome, but also a joke intended to make me smile. And it worked, but it also makes me cringe in hindsight because I know now how that term was used to exclude thousands of evacuees from the rhetoric of citizenship, from the discourse of belonging to their country and deserving assistance from it. I also know now how far I was from the risks of actually being seen as a refugee, as so many people of color who fled New Orleans were seen. And so this memory becomes painful in a new way, as it reminds me not only of my emotional state during evacuation but of the protection that in that vulnerable moment I was granted, while others were not.

Folklorist Frank De Caro (2013) describes how he generally tells two stories about his relatively privileged experience of displacement. The first is about the fear he and his wife felt as they faced the possibility of not being able to find gas while evacuating. The second recalls the luxurious apartment of a friend, where they stayed until they could return to New Orleans. De Caro explains that he tells these two tales "as if I need one story that says our exile was mostly a painless one and another to highlight the difficult uncertainties of the experience" (200). My selection of stories generally reflects a similar desire, both to convey the hardships I felt and to qualify my suffering in light of the extremes endured by others. But what I find most important, more so than the particular stories that De Caro tells or that I tell, is the fact of our selective narration: we have the ability to choose how we share our hurricane experiences, to influence how audiences will perceive us. This is not always the case for those whose disaster stories get carried away and told by others.

My professional work since Katrina has been primarily devoted to figuring out how the stories of other survivors are told, how they are changed through the course of their circulation to wide audiences, and how their reception influences public perception and recovery efforts; I summarize some of these trends below but examine them in more detail elsewhere (Horigan 2018). In general, though the public demand for personal narratives of traumatic experience might seem beneficial to those who have such stories to tell, the reception of those narratives is ultimately harmful for survivors. Publishers recognize that people want to put an individual face on massive disasters; understandably, the scale of such events is difficult to comprehend without feeling some sort of personal connection. The way in which that personal connection is generally cultivated, though, is artificial and injurious: personal stories are stripped of their complexities and presented to audiences in oversimplified forms with which they feel comfortable. For example, in his bestseller *Zeitoun*, Dave Eggers (2009) crafts the personal recollections of Katrina survivor Abdulrahman Zeitoun into a polished story of heroism. Zeitoun assisted neighbors during the flooding of New Orleans and was then wrongfully imprisoned because first responders suspected him of terrorism. Eggers thoughtfully examines the confluence of America's foreign policy and domestic disaster response, showing how Islamophobia went unchecked in post-Katrina confusion. Comparing Eggers's book to previous versions of Zeitoun's story, however, reveals that as a narrator Zeitoun presents much more ambiguity about his actions than Eggers conveys. Subsequent events also confirm that Zeitoun is a dynamic individual, capable of both heroic acts and villainous ones; he is currently serving a prison sentence for violent offenses against his family. This is not simply a case of Eggers being mistaken about Zeitoun's true character, though. Rather, it is a pattern in the publication of personal disaster narratives, where stories are made to fit dominant narratives, reducing the people they describe to stereotypes.

Stereotyping happens to a much lesser extent when narrators are involved in the publication of their stories and when that involvement is incorporated into the final, published product. For instance, the documentary *Trouble the Water* includes, as described above, extraordinary flood footage shot by Kim Roberts. As viewers of the documentary watch these clips, they also hear Roberts's commentary about the process of recording them and her anticipation of possibly being able to sell her video to "white folks." The inclusion of such metacommentary in the film itself helps disrupt the depiction of Roberts as a helpless African American victim, an all-too-common misrepresentation of people devastated by the storm in New Orleans. Similarly, in comic artist Josh Neufeld's (2009) *A.D.: New Orleans after the Deluge*, the presentation of a real-life survivor, Denise, turns into a stereotypical depiction of an angry Black woman. When this text was published as a webcomic, however, Denise had the opportunity to negotiate the context of her story's reception in online comments (Neufeld 2007–8). There, much like Kim Roberts, she interrupts the reduction of her complex experiences by challenging readers' interpretations of her words and actions. These cases indicate a hopeful pattern: when survivors share their stories, they attempt to control how those stories are heard, as I do when sharing my experiences and as the participants in SKRH did in their interviews. When those negotiations are erased in the publication of personal narratives, the narratives slide into stereotype, resulting in a reductive portrayal of complex people and communities. As a result, recovery efforts are hampered; for example, if New Orleanians are seen as angry, they are viewed as a threat to first responders. If they are seen as helpless, their own expertise is not sought in recovery plans. When narrators' efforts to influence reception are included in their story as it is shared, though, audiences get a fuller picture of survivors. This fuller picture is essential to developing effective, survivor-centered responses to disasters.

Conclusion

Elizabeth Fussell (2008, 65) describes the unique knowledge and position of survivor-scholars: "Social scientists residing in a community can be valuable resources for rebuilding: They know the community well, they observe what is occurring on the ground, they are more likely to be trusted by residents, and they have credibility with outside observers as well as community members. . . . By being both the subject and object of their own research, they gain invaluable scholarly insight."

I hope that the type of insight I share in scholarly venues, regarding the public circulation of survivors' personal narratives, will ultimately increase survivors' command over their stories and the recovery of their communities. I also recognize that these insights are gained at a cost. In part, that cost is personal, and it includes the pain of Katrina and the emotional labor required to continue remembering and writing about it. Fussell's (2008, 65) description of doing Katrina-centered work from far away resonates with me: "An advantage of studying New Orleans from a distance is that I can choose my research topics more intentionally and not explore every possible topic that presents itself and on which I have some degree of expertise. Furthermore, I can decide when I am at work and when I am not, rather than living in it." But this is also the most disconcerting cost of this sort of work for me, a constant awareness of my privilege with respect to it: I was able to leave, and I am able to choose, for the most part, not to live constantly in the anxiety of ongoing trauma, even when it is the subject of my work. I am building a career based on observing hardship—my own, but also that of others. I have attempted to examine and embrace this difficult position more fully here, though, because I believe that its combination of suffering and distance is a valuable vantage point for disaster scholarship and recovery.

Amy Shuman (2005, 149) has written that "ethnographers who attempt to describe suffering have as their greatest task the critique of empathy," wherein empathy is understood as potentially self-serving, a means by which suffering becomes sensational, consumable, and detached from those who endure it. I suggest that being both survivor and ethnographer provides a unique perspective from which such a critique of empathy may be launched. When I share the uncomfortable bits of my own story here, it is in the interest of deromanticizing personal narratives of disaster. I do not wish to share only those pieces that will create an empathetic response. I also share the pieces that represent my privilege, the aspects of my experience that position me in relationship to other narratives of Katrina survival: not fully the "me too" stories that Shuman (2005, 60) identifies, but rather a partial and limited identification. Similarly, when other survivors' narratives are shared, they must have this opportunity for engagement. As Shuman (2005, 25) says regarding narratives of suffering, "The problem is not the accuracy of representations but the relationship between listeners and tellers produced by those representations." For many Katrina survivors, especially working-class African Americans, the representations that dominated public discourse created relationships of distrust: survivors were seen either as not deserving of empathy and not to be trusted because they were dangerous or as deserving of empathy but not to be trusted with resources for recovery because they were helpless. When survivors' critiques of how their narratives are shared reach the audiences for those narratives, the possibility for listeners' self-serving empathy is greatly reduced. In the process of becoming a survivor-ethnographer, I have recognized that telling and listening to Katrina stories produces a relationship of distance between myself and other survivors. Although that distance has been painful at times, in that it makes ownership of my own suffering difficult, I believe it has also enabled a different kind of perspective—the critical kind—that underscores that which I do not know and understand when it comes to the traumatic experiences of others. This distance characterizes the critical empathy with which ethnographic and official responses to disasters should begin; its isolation cries out for the expert knowledge of other survivors.

Note

1. For more on SKRH, see chap. 1.

References

Barber, Kristen. 2007. "The Emotional Management of a Stranger: Negotiating Class Privilege and Masculine Academics as a Hurricane Katrina Evacuee." In *Narrating the Storm: Sociological Stories of Hurricane Katrina*, edited by Danielle Antoinette Hidalgo and Kristen Barber, 78–89. Newcastle: Cambridge Scholars Publishing.

Borland, Katherine. 1998. "'That's Not What I Said': Interpretive Conflict in Oral Narrative Research." In *Women's Words: The Feminist Practice of Oral History*, edited by Sherna Berger Gluck and Daphne Patai, 63–76. New York: Routledge.

Deal, Carl, and Tia Lessen, dirs. 2008. *Trouble the Water*. New York: Zeitgeist Films.

De Caro, Frank. 2013. "Katrina: We Leave, We Return, Stories Abound." In *Stories of Our Lives: Memory, History, Narrative*, 198–209. Logan: Utah State University Press.

Eggers, Dave. 2009. *Zeitoun*. San Francisco: McSweeney's.

Fussell, Elizabeth. 2008. "Leaving New Orleans, Again." *Traumatology* 14 (4): 63–66.

Grider, Sylvia. 2001. "Spontaneous Shrines: A Modern Response to Tragedy and Disaster." *New Directions in Folklore* 5: 1–8.

Haney, Timothy J., and Kristen Barber. 2013. "Reconciling Academic Objectivity and Subjective Trauma: The Double Consciousness of Sociologists Who Experienced Hurricane Katrina." *Critical Sociology* 39 (1): 105–22.

Hidalgo, Danielle Antoinette. 2007. "Introduction: Storytelling Sociology." In *Narrating the Storm: Sociological Stories of Hurricane Katrina*, edited by Danielle Antoinette Hidalgo and Kristen Barber, 1–9. Newcastle: Cambridge Scholars Publishing.

Horigan, Kate Parker. 2018. *Consuming Katrina: Public Disaster and Personal Narrative.* Jackson: University Press of Mississippi.

Lawless, Elaine. 1992. "'I Was Afraid Someone Like You . . . an Outsider . . . Would Misunderstand': Negotiating Interpretive Differences between Ethnographers and Subjects." *Journal of American Folklore* 105 (417): 302–14.

Lindahl, Carl. 2012. "Legends of Hurricane Katrina: The Right to Be Wrong, Survivor-to-Survivor Storytelling, and Healing." *Journal of American Folklore* 125 (496): 139–76.

Neufeld, Josh. 2007–8. *A.D.: New Orleans after the Deluge. SMITHMag.net.* http://www.smithmag.net/afterthedeluge/.

———. 2009. *A.D.: New Orleans after the Deluge.* New York: Pantheon.

Sánchez-Carretero, Cristina. 2011. "The Madrid Train Bombings: Enacting the Emotional Body at the March 11 Grassroots Memorials." In *Grassroots Memorials: The Politics of Memorializing Traumatic Death*, edited by Peter Jan Margry and Cristina Sánchez-Carretero, 244–61. New York: Berghahn Books.

Sánchez-Carretero, Cristina, and Carmen Ortiz. 2008. "Rethinking Ethnology in the Spanish Context." *Ethnologia Europaea* 38 (1): 23–28.

Shuman, Amy. 2005. *Other People's Stories: Entitlement Claims and the Critique of Empathy.* Champaign: University of Illinois Press.

Turner, Kay. 2009. "September 11th: The Burden of the Ephemeral." *Western Folklore* 68 (2/3): 155–208.

Zeitlin, Steve. 2006. "Oh Did You See the Ashes Come Thickly Falling Down? Poems Posted in the Wake of September 11." In *Spontaneous Shrines and the Public Memorialization of Death*, edited by Jack Santino, 99–117. New York: Palgrave Macmillan.

Kate Parker HORIGAN is Associate Professor in the Department of Folk Studies and Anthropology at Western Kentucky University. She is author of *Consuming Katrina: Public Disaster and Personal Narrative* (2018). kate.horigan@wku.edu.

6

EMPATHY AND SPEAKING OUT

Amy Shuman

Trauma elicits a response, and folklorists have created a very particular kind of response, born out of our capacity and commitment to listen to others. It's tempting to call this response empathy, and although the desire for empathy, the desire to comprehend the tragedies experienced by others with compassion, is part of what motivates the commitment to listen, I want to suggest a few cautions here and to recommend that we instead maintain the more modest, but ultimately more productive, stance of listening and recognizing the inevitable imbalances produced in engagements between people who have experienced traumatic events and people willing to serve as witnesses to those accounts. In this chapter, I suggest that the field of folklore makes a contribution to our understanding of empathy in two directions. First, as a matter of methods, folklorists and ethnographers more generally understand the imbalances created by encounters between people whose cultural practices are unfamiliar to each other. Understanding others has been a foundational methodological principle of ethnographic research from its inception; when one is faced with the inevitable imbalances, the remedy is not only to study within one's familiar group; instead, methodologies such as those discussed in this book offer possibilities for cross-cultural research. Second, as part of narrative research, folklorists have identified some of the limits of tellability. Where methodology turns our attention to the challenges faced by the researcher in cross-cultural research, narrative analysis turns our attention to the challenges faced by the teller, by the person who experiences the trauma. By combining these two directions, the methodological challenges of the researcher and the tellability challenges of the narrator, folklore provides a dialogic approach to empathy.

As a folklorist studying narratives told by people applying for political asylum, I am confronted by both dimensions of the problem of empathy. To receive asylum, applicants have to describe indescribable, sometimes humiliating experiences in a process that often forces them into the realm of what would be untellable in their home communities. And as a listener, I know that I cannot fully comprehend what they have experienced, and although I recognize the conditions of untellability, to help them create a strong case, I need to persuade them to find a way to describe what has happened to them. In a review of the Netflix series *Orange Is the New Black*, Emily Nussbaum (2016, 86) writes that the theme of the show "has always been empathy, a refusal to see anyone as inhuman." Nussbaum complicates this refusal, presumably on the part of the writers, by considering the diverse characters and audiences and the gulf they might try to traverse. Writing about the controversial (for fans) death of one of the characters, she states, "This season's smartest move was to interrogate empathy rather than treating it as a cure-all. Compassion is a resource, too. Who gets it and who gets cut off?" (87). In my work, I have been interested in how folklorists might interrogate empathy, not only as a resource that might be unevenly distributed but also as part of the often unfulfilled promise of narrative to provide understanding across gaps and gulfs (Shuman 2006). If empathy is a remedy, then, I suggest, it is better understood dialogically, as a response that connects a narrator and listener and includes the possibility of witnessing an untellable narrative. In this chapter, I first consider the different disciplinary legacies brought to the concept of empathy and then return to the study of trauma narrative in a human rights tribunal. I conclude with an account of a strategic, or critical, approach to empathy.

Origins of the Concept of Empathy

The concept of empathy is often attributed to Hermann Lotze and Robert Vischer's conception of *Einfühlung*, a German term meaning "feeling into," which was adapted in English by Edward B. Titchener, who termed it *empathy*.[1] Heinz Kohut (1959) introduced the term to psychoanalysis. As differentiated from the concepts of sympathy or compassion, which suggest recognition of someone else's suffering, empathy adds the idea of understanding suffering from the sufferer's point of view. Sympathy is usually associated with a discourse of sentimentalism also associated with pity. Samuel Moyn (2006, 402) writes, "Only after and because sentimental humanitarianism came to be the moral horizon of modern times could the fact that most people are insufficiently sensitive to the pains and traumas of others begin to seem deplorable. Empathy, one might say, has always ruled through its threatened or realized absence." In other words, the concept of empathy is part of a discourse of expectation and repair. Empathy is one way to acknowledge the suffering of others.

Unlike the eighteenth- and nineteenth-century discourses on sympathy, twentieth- and twenty-first-century discourses acknowledge the companion problems of compassion fatigue and voyeurism.[2] Both concepts call attention to the relationship between the witness and the person who has experienced trauma, and both point to ways that the witness can either fail to respond or exploit the relationship. Importantly, discussions of empathy point not only to the recognition of human resilience but also to the recognition of human frailty (Moyn 2006, 404). And sometimes resilience and frailty are in contradiction to each other. They can represent different values. This is especially the case when the measure of empathy is used as a measure of humanity. I will return to this issue as the problem of equating empathy with redemption.

Empathy in Ethnographic Research

The many anthropologists and linguistic anthropologists who have examined specific cultural, communicative contexts to comprehend local understandings of empathy have provided a rich source of inquiry (Hollan and Throop 2008). All seem to agree on a definition of empathy as a first-person-like perspective on another that involves an emotional, embodied, or experiential aspect (391–92).

In ethnographic research, the concept of empathy is also closely related to that of intersubjectivity. Douglas Hollan and C. Jason Throop's work summarizes and interrogates recent work and also revisits Clifford Geertz's (1984 [1976]) critique of empathy, "in which he used the failure of anthropologists and others to distinguish clearly between empathy and projection to challenge the idea that gaining first-person-like knowledge of others involves any kind of special experiential or emotional component" (2008, 388). After reviewing the debates and positions about empathy, Hollan and Throop write, "One thing that is clear from the limited anthropological literature currently available is that first-person-like knowledge of others in the context of everyday social practice is rarely, if ever, considered an unambiguously good thing despite the many positive connotations empathy has in the North American context. Although such knowledge may be used to help others or to interact with them more effectively, it may also be used to hurt or embarrass them. Because of this, people all over the world seem just as concerned with concealing their first-person-subjective experience from others as in revealing it" (389).

Not surprisingly, Geertz's pronouncement on anthropological approaches to empathy is part of a discussion of the role of the anthropologist in the field. Writing about what were at that time recent revelations of Malinowski's diaries, Geertz (1975, 47) said, "The myth of the chameleon fieldworker perfectly self-attuned to his exotic surroundings—a walking miracle of empathy, tact, patience, and cosmopolitanism—was demolished by the man who had perhaps done the most to create it." For Geertz, the important question at stake is anthropology's "injunction to see things from the native's point of view" (47). Using the German terms, he writes, "What happens to verstehen when einfühlen disappears?" (47). Geertz goes on to talk about the distinction, borrowed from Heinz Kohut, between experience-near and experience-distant concepts. Kohut is the same scholar who introduced the concept of empathy; it is not an accidental connection. Geertz does not quote Kohut on empathy, but he does critique the concept as based on a Western concept of self.

After describing very different senses of self in Bali, Java, and Morocco, Geertz concludes his essay by suggesting, though he doesn't say so in so many words, that the anthropologist doesn't really need a concept of empathy. He writes, "Understanding the form and pressure of, to use the dangerous word one more time, natives' inner lives is more like grasping a proverb, catching an allusion, seeing a joke—or, as I have suggested, reading a poem—than it is like achieving communion" (1975, 53).

Can anthropological or ethnographic understanding be helpful for understanding interpersonal understanding? Vincent Crapanzano (1981, 352) is critical of Geertz's use of both the metaphor of grasping a proverb and of Kohut's distinction between experience-near and experience-distant, which he regards as "not altogether well thought out." Crapanzano describes Geertz as "'spiralling' between a presumptive phenomenological perspective . . . and an interpretive stance. . . . At times . . . Geertz assumes the 'experience-near' perspective of his informants (without presenting the evidence for his assumptions) and at other times he writes descriptively ('experience-distantly') from his 'objective' point of view" (858–59). "Experience-near" is clearly not the solution if it is an impressionistic account purporting to be an insider's view.

As this discussion—in which Crapanzano takes on Geertz, who situates himself in the debates about Malinowski—reveals, discussions about empathy and ethnography are not new. Almost everyone who engages in discussions of empathy situates the discussion within some form of historical cultural baggage that needs to be untangled. As Samuel Moyn (2006, 415) says, "Empathy, whatever its novelty, thus remains subject to old accusations."

Empathy and Trauma Research

Discussions of empathy are often an appeal to recognize the humanity of others in response to the failure to do so. Thus Dori Laub and Nanette C. Auerhahn (1989, 379) refer to what they describe as "the failure of empathy . . . a massive failure of the interpersonal environment to mediate needs. . . . It is as if the victim's messages were sent into outer space. Such lack of receptivity can only occur when the person experiencing and expressing the wish is not regarded as equally human." In their essay, Laub and Auerhahn describe the obliterating effects of genocide (specifically the Holocaust) and the possibilities afforded by therapy. In their study of Holocaust survivors, Laub and Auerhahn describe the defining feature of trauma in which others have attempted to deliberately destroy individuals as the "violation or impairment of the internal representation of the link between self and other. This link is predicated on the expectation of mutual responsiveness and empathy—the expectation that the other can and will respond to and satisfy one's basic needs. . . . At its most extreme, trauma results in complete severing of the link between self and other" (397). As Carl Lindahl's (2012, 152–59) survivor-to-survivor project and others in this issue confirm, listening can work to restore the link that has been severed between self and other, and restoring this link is crucial.

In Dominick LaCapra's (1999) work, as in the work of many others, the Holocaust presents the limits that make some sorts of experiences and their tellings unintelligible, both necessary to understand and, at the same time, defying understanding. LaCapra introduces the concept of "empathic unsettlement" to describe the relationship between the teller and listener. He writes, "The role of empathy and empathic unsettlement in the attentive secondary witness . . . involves a kind of virtual experience through which one puts oneself in the other's position while recognizing the difference of that position and hence not taking the other's place. Opening oneself to empathic unsettlement is, as I intimated, a desirable affective dimension of inquiry that complements and supplements empirical research and analysis" (722–23).

Empathy in Psychological Research

More recently, psychologists have become interested in empathy among both humans and animals (Eisenberg and Strayer 1987; Kirmayer 2008). Defining *empathy* more broadly, as the ability "to quickly and automatically relate to the emotional states of others," psychologists such as Frans B. M. de Waal (2008, 282) regard empathy as "essential for the regulation of social interactions, coordinated activity, and cooperation toward shared goals." In other words, *empathy* can refer to "emotional connectedness" as well as an "appraisal of the other's situation and attempts to understand the cause of the other's emotions" (283). These more basic empathic responses are differentiated from what de Waal refers to as "perspective taking" or "adoption of the other's point of view" (285). This higher level of empathy has been observed in several social animal encounters, among primates helping one another, among elephants comforting distressed companions, and across species. To expand on these observations in the animal world, then, we can say that a lack of empathy not only dehumanizes but also refuses any fundamental connection. Empathy in human hands represents complex relationships between self and other, perhaps especially evident in discourses about disability where what might look like compassion actually breaks bonds of connection. Research on empathy beyond the human is most useful when it considers, in Nussbaum's terms, the conditions for distributing and withholding compassion, as well as the price (86).

Empathy in Disability Studies

Reviews of the combined discourses of pity and inspiration in disability studies research are enormously helpful for understanding the possibilities and limits of empathy. Describing the typical poster creating pity for disabled people, Joseph Shapiro (1993, 12) writes, "The poster child is a sure-fire tug at our hearts. The children picked to represent charity fundraising drives are brave, determined, and inspirational, the most innocent victims of the cruelest whims of life and health. . . . No other symbol of disability is more beloved by Americans than the cute and courageous poster child—or more loathed by people with disabilities themselves."

As Shapiro notes, disabled people speak back to the poster; their loathing constitutes a form of critique more formalized in the disability rights movement that Shapiro and others chronicle. In contrast to the conditions for empathy described by Laub and Auerhahn and employed by Lindahl and others in this volume, the inspirational poster obliterates the connection between self and other. Disabled people often emphatically refuse empathy and observe that empathy comes with a price, in the form of either pity or victimization. Even (or especially) purportedly positive claims of admiration or inspiration are distancing and dehumanizing, creating a high bar for recognition of those who overcome the challenges they face and, by implication, refusing recognition for those who do not.

As most scholars writing about empathy have observed, when empathy is one-directional (as in the poster), it reinstantiates, rather than reduces, difference.[3]

Empathy and Literary Fiction

Examinations of empathy in literature have attended primarily to the problem of how works of fiction describe relationships among characters and then might invite readers to identify with those connections (Gubar 2002). For example, Suzanne Keen (2006, 215) differentiates among "bounded strategic empathy," which "operates within an in-group, stemming from experiences of mutuality and leading to feeling with familiar others"; "ambassadorial strategic empathy," which "addresses chosen others with the aim of cultivating their empathy for the in-group often to a specific end"; and "broadcast strategic empathy," which "calls upon every reader to feel with members of a group, by emphasizing common vulnerabilities and hopes through universalizing representations." Keen is interested in character identification and reader response, problems closer to those of the ethnographer studying cross-culturally than to the questions of tellability raised by LaCapra and Laub and Auerhahn.

In a postmodern discussion of empathy, Michael Roemer (1995, 247) argues that empathy's opposite is alienation and that one cannot exist without the other. "Verfremdung [alienation] is but one polarity of the aesthetic experience, and meaningless without its opposite—Einfühlung, or empathy."

Further, Roemer writes, "Robbed of irony, narrative becomes monopolar and sentimental" (244). Indeed, although many scholars writing about empathy focus concern on the impossibilities of understanding (as I have here), the more complex discussion must include the relationship between empathy and disinterest. If the danger of a simple concept of empathy—suggesting that it is possible to walk in another's shoes or that doing so will produce compassion—is the sentimental, then the further danger is compassion fatigue.[4]

Empathy and Folklore Research

I have argued that the concept of empathy is most useful as an understanding of the *limits* of as well as the capacity for understanding others (Shuman 2005). As folklorists, we are accustomed to viewing culture as the obstacle to understanding across difference. Culture as a lived, embodied experience of daily, symbolic, and political life is specific and contextual; it cannot be generalized, nor do people necessarily articulate the fundamental, taken-for-granted understandings that govern their interpretations. As the folklorists in this collection have observed, trauma disturbs those patterns of cultural life, sometimes permanently. If ordinary life was ever intelligible, even if unarticulated, trauma can make it unintelligible, unrecognizable, unfathomable. The task, then, often is to empathize with the loss of ordinary life. Even survivors, having shared a collective trauma, often say that they cannot speak for one another or that they cannot speak for a collective whole. To some extent, the representation of trauma is always about the unrepresentable, the untellable, the unspeakable. And yet, at the same time, the obligation to remember, to tell, and the desire to be heard supersede this limitation.

The inquiry about empathy then requires us to attend to the gap in our understanding of others' experiences. It is not only about how we bridge that gap but also about how we recognize it as a gap. In my earlier research, I was interested in what happens when stories travel beyond the contexts of the people whose lives they describe and especially in what kinds of cross-context understanding are claimed through the transmission of these stories. I encountered many examples of people who claimed to be able to understand the vastly different experiences, especially traumatic experiences, of others through hearing their stories. Also, I collected examples of people who felt that their stories had been misappropriated and misunderstood by others. I described this second pattern as the limits of empathy and proposed, as an alternative, the kind of critical empathy that Dominick LaCapra describes as empathic unsettlement.

Empathy and Speaking Out in a Human Rights Tribunal

The companion to empathic listening is tellability. In the simplest sense—and of course such exchanges are never simple, just as they are never completely reciprocal—empathic listening affords tellability. A sympathetic listener, someone predisposed to hear what the teller has to say, is one condition for telling what are otherwise difficult and even taboo topics. Carl Lindahl's (2012) project is designed to create these conditions. His work, and that of others associated with the survivor-to-survivor project, has deepened our understanding of how this works.

Building on that work, I offer another example here, from the film *The Uncondemned*, which documents how a group of Tutsi women were able to testify to an international tribunal about being raped during the Rwandan genocide (Mitchell 2015). Their testimonies resulted in the first successful prosecution of rape as a war crime in an international tribunal. I use this example because, as a film, it is available for readers to gain a fuller understanding of the complexity of tellability than I can provide with a narrative transcript. The women's discussion of rape corresponds to my own research with political asylum applicants. My coauthor, Carol Bohmer, and I frequently have encountered applicants who have been reluctant to talk about humiliations, especially stigmatized sexual violations, that they experienced. Since the Tutsi women depicted in the film chose to make their stories public, I do not violate privacy by further exposing someone's already precarious telling.

On September 2, 1998, the International Criminal Tribunal for Rwanda (a United Nations court) convicted Jean-Paul Akayesu, mayor of the Rwandan town of Taba, of rape as part of the Rwandan genocide. This was the first international conviction of rape as a human rights violation. As *The Uncondemned* relates, one of the women from the village of Taba prayed that if her husband and children would be spared in the genocide, she would devote herself to serving Christ. They did survive, and after the war, she looked for a path for her service and decided to create a women's group to talk about what they had suffered. Rape was a taboo topic; women who had been raped were already stigmatized. The tribunals were hesitant to prosecute for this reason.

Binaifer Nowrojee (1996), whose account of the atrocities for Human Rights Watch provided important evidence for the tribunal, reports: "The Deputy Prosecutor of the Rwandan Tribunal told Human Rights Watch/ FIDH that the reason they have not collected rape testimonies is because 'African women don't want to talk about rape. We haven't received any real complaints. It's rare in investigations that women refer to rape.' As this report indicates, if interviews are conducted in conditions of safety and privacy, and if Rwandan women believe that telling their testimony will help bring about justice, they will talk."

The women's group solicited the help of a social worker to facilitate their grieving, and, slowly, they described having been raped. Here the women's narratives join a different narrative thread: the unsuccessful efforts of nongovernmental organization (NGO) human rights workers to document and prosecute rape as part of war.

The women's personal testimonies served to document international crimes against humanity, creating an intersection between personal and political narrative and a confluence of Western and Rwandan values and agendas. The film gains its force from these personal stories, mapped onto a political narrative. The film intertwines the stories of the Rwandan women from Taba with the stories of the NGO activists and lawyers, and here we can ask whether we have more identification if not empathy with the political narrative. Further, do we lose sight of the cultural cost to the women for whom political agency might mean an alliance with Western values that, in some circumstances, criticize or obliterate cultural traditional values? This is one of the areas, often overlooked, in which folklorists can contribute understanding.

The Rwandan women had to be persuaded to testify; they were well aware of the consequences of making their story public and of the fact that success was not guaranteed, to say the least. Testifying required them to expose themselves to shame, an exposure with consequences not only for themselves but also for their families. Further, they traveled a great distance, outside their geographic and social comfort zones, to be subjected to a legal inquiry where they faced less than sympathetic listeners. In the film, the Western NGO officers prepare them and accompany them, but still, they are speaking far outside their cultural milieu, and to what ends? They cannot undo the suffering they have experienced, and we need to ask whether vindication in an international context can provide some sort of repair.

The question of the possibilities of repair is at the heart of occasions like UN tribunals, truth and reconciliation hearings, and the survivor-to-survivor project. As the Tutsi women report at the end of the film, vindication—and making history—does serve as a kind of repair, and, as they say, in this case, speaking out has its own rewards. As many feminist scholars have observed, speaking out can change gendered social hierarchies. Speaking out, especially against the silences imposed by taboo, can, but does not necessarily, disrupt those taboos. The Tutsi women depicted in the film viewed their choice to speak out as a collective liberatory act. Their testimonies were not just personal stories. Each woman told her personal story, and each struggled with the choice to tell and the difficulty of speaking at all. They made those choices in the context of a collective action of solidarity with one another, as part of their local village group. For viewers of the film, their story represents a larger story of vindication and history-making prosecution of human rights violations.

Legal uses of personal narratives and testimonies often have competing ethical concerns. *The Uncondemned* depicts the different agendas of the participants only briefly, in interchanges between the NGOs and the Rwandan women. For the most part, they occupy two parallel narrative universes in the film. For the policy makers and human rights activists, the Rwandan women's experiences are an example of a larger pattern of human rights violations against women. In the film, the shared purposes of the women and the human rights activists successfully compete against the complicity that fostered the human rights violations. As the film documents, the groundbreaking international conviction of rape as a human rights violation was made possible by a rare confluence of factors. Jean-Paul Akayesu, the mayor of the village, who is on trial, and who has argued that he did not commit the rapes himself, is convicted of knowing about and failing to prevent them and thus facilitating the human rights violations. As the mayor of a small town, he was, perhaps, less protected by powerful interests and thus more vulnerable to a tribunal. His conviction was made possible when a group of women, otherwise silenced by their own local taboos against speaking, broke through the stigma and chose to speak publicly. This confluence of factors and different complicities reveals also the conflicting ethical commitments that are found in any human rights endeavor and that are central to a remedy to the deep and powerful fissures between self and other caused by human rights violations.

Empathy, one remedy to these fissures, is replete with a surplus of ethical commitments. The women from Taba decided to speak, to tell what were untellable humiliations and violations to their human integrity, even though doing so exposed them to public stigma. Their willingness to tell their stories made it possible for others, far beyond their circumstances, to hear them and act on them, resulting not only in empathy but also a shared ethical commitment to justice.

Empathy is not promised in legal proceedings, such as the UN tribunal or political asylum hearings, which are, primarily, inquiries. Although the tribunals and political asylum hearing testimonies include stories of some of the worst human rights violations, of suffering, of being torn away from family and home, and of the complete destruction of ordinary life, the exchange is not about compassion. Although motivated by a desire for justice and even by compassion, legal hearings, especially political asylum proceedings, are designed to ferret out those lacking credibility or those whose cases do not warrant refuge as defined by international and national policies. Speaking out, then, produces precarity as often as it produces remediation.

Conclusion

Empathy has emerged in the discourses of the twentieth and twenty-first centuries in part as a response to failures to exercise it. For example, contemporary political asylum policy, created after World War II, is an attempt to remedy a colossal humanitarian failure. Empathy, then, is part of a dialogue, a response that requires attention to the suffering of others, including attention to the difficulty or even impossibility of narrating it. Here we return to the connection between empathy and tellability as questions of who can listen and who can tell and as a response to a call to remedy a break. Empathic listening—or, to return to LaCapra's term, empathic unsettlement—calls attention to the gaps in understanding others and to the gaps of violence creating a break between self and other. Underlying the possibilities of empathy are the frameworks of structural violence that can be too easily overlooked by frameworks of compassion. The personal and political stories are deeply implicated in these frameworks of structural violence.

In other work, I've described this connection between the personal story and the larger story, in which the personal story represents a larger shared experience, as allegorical (Shuman 2006). The personal story as allegorical message acquires a different, but not lesser force, with a different set of obligations and relationships among tellers and listeners. I use the term *allegorical* to signal the difference. It is not just a matter of scale. As Walter Benjamin (1977, 177–78) famously wrote, "Allegories are in the realm of thoughts what ruins are in the realm of things" (see also Gelley 1999).

Like ruins, allegories are inevitably partial. They are not a small story writ large or a personal story shared by many. Nor is the shift from personal to shared merely a matter of distortion. If anything, the allegory is too much of the same. When one person's story becomes everyone's story, or the reverse, the similarity can become overdetermined, imposing repetition and sameness that can be comforting or disarming. Allegories as ruins contain a longing for something whole, and the personal account is rarely a perfect match to that whole. Instead, the partiality of allegory always interrupts itself.

Empathy is part of a process of transmission of both stories that demand to be told and experiences that are fundamentally uncommunicable.[5] In other words, empathy has the task of bridging unbridgeable distances. It is this distance that I have discussed in earlier work and that I want to return to here. My concern in my earlier writing about empathy is what has often been called overidentification, a failure to see the difference between one's own feelings and perceptions and those of the person whose suffering one witnesses. I remain concerned about the possibilities of exploitation afforded by the appropriation of others' suffering, a concern everyone in this volume shares. In my earlier work, I referred to "easy empathy," but the issue may perhaps be more accurately described by Bertold Brecht's term "crude empathy," as it is not the ease of overidentification that is the problem but instead the obliteration of a possible connection, as in the case of inspirational representations of disability. Empathy requires being willing to be taken in by someone else's experiences (a practice not far from the project of fieldwork in general) and being a witness to both the experiences recounted and the unbridgeable and yet possibly sustaining connections created. It is a necessary and insufficient response to trauma, as much about commensurability as about incommensurability.[6]

Afterword, Added in 2021

In this chapter on the possibilities and limitations for telling and understanding stories about trauma, I suggested that tellability is a companion to empathetic listening. I think the chapters in this volume suggest a stronger statement: empathetic listening *requires* attention to tellability. Both Carl Lindahl (chap. 1) and Kate Parker Horigan (chap. 5) advocate for survivors having control of their own stories. Similarly, ownership of their stories was crucial for the women portrayed in *The Uncondemned*. For the Rwandan women, as for many of the survivors described in this volume, telling and being heard (having empathetic listeners) is connected.

In this update, I want to add an additional point. Although the stories people tell following disasters sometimes *describe* resilience, neither telling nor listening necessarily *provides* a sense of resilience. While sharing stories about disasters may build community and facilitate a sense of resilience, resilience cannot be imposed. In fact, imposing the message of resilience can take away control of one's own story. Michael Dylan Foster (chap. 7) observes how resilience can be experienced in a different form, such as in the "lightness" of control over a local ritual, and how control over the ritual might be a corollary to telling one's own story.

My own engagement with questions of tellability and empathy is personal, in two ways. First, I learned about tellability from my aunt, who was in hiding during World War II. As a twelve-year-old child, she fled with her grandmother from Paris when the Nazis deported Jews, and they lived in a storage shed in the town of Voiron. I didn't know much about my aunt's story, except that she lived in fear and that her mother died in Auschwitz. My aunt didn't regard her story as tellable until 1998, when she was interviewed by the Shoah Foundation. In part, she didn't regard herself as a "Holocaust survivor," since she had not been in a camp. She now tells it regularly, as a member of the speaker bureau of the Holocaust Museum in Washington, D.C. Like the participants in Surviving Katrina and Rita in Houston, my aunt found empathetic listeners in others who had shared her experience. However, in telling her story, she does not seek or gain resilience. Instead, she feels an obligation to tell it, to share the truth of her experience (not unlike the Katrina survivors).

My second personal engagement with tellability and empathy is my resistance to the expectation of becoming resilient sometimes imposed by others in regard to disability. Disability is not trauma or disaster. But it does provide an example of another situation in which it's important to tell one's own story. My youngest son has disabilities, which I've written about elsewhere. Like others living with, or adjacent to, disability, I found that empathy often came with a suggestion, even a demand, for compulsory resilience. In a deft sleight of hand, our personal story of living our new form of ordinary life became someone else's story of resilience. Empathetic listening requires the listener to avoid imposing a message, even a positive message of resilience.

Notes

1. See Theodore Lipps's (1979) discussion of Lotze, Vischer, and Titchener. See also Boltanski (1999); Spector (1998); Stein (1989).

2. The term *compassion fatigue* was originally used to refer to people in social work fields who helped trauma victims (Deering 1996).

3. See also phenomenological approaches to empathy (Csordas 1990) and linguistic anthropological studies of autism (Ochs et al. 2004).

4. See for example the video "Empathy: The Human Connection to Patient Care," which begins with a quote from H. D. Thoreau and then portrays patients and something about their travails at the hospital (Cleveland Clinic n.d.). It ends with the question, "If you could stand in someone's shoes, hear what they hear, see what they see, would you treat them differently?" It is a tearjerker, a moving video that would make most viewers sad. But is this sadness understanding?

5. See also Marianne Hirsch's (2002, 73) discussion of postmemory as partial and as motivated by the generational break between those who suffered and their children, who become witnesses "who were not there to live it but who received its effects, belatedly through the narratives, actions, and symptoms of the previous generation, trauma both solidifies and blurs generational difference."

6. For a discussion of anthropology and incommensurability, see Povinelli (2001).

References

Benjamin, Walter. 1977. *The Origin of German Tragic Drama*. London: New Left Books.

Boltanski, Luc. 1999. *Distant Suffering: Morality, Media and Politics*. Cambridge: Cambridge University Press.

Cleveland Clinic. n.d. "Empathy: The Human Connection to Patient Care." YouTube. https://www.youtube.com/watch?v=cDDWvj_q-08.

Crapanzano, Vincent. 1981. Review of *Meaning and Order in Moroccan Society: Three Essays in Cultural Analysis (with a Photographic Essay by Paul Hyman)*, by Clifford Geertz, Hildred Geertz, and Lawrence Rosen. *Economic Development and Cultural Change* 29 (4): 849–60.

Csordas, Thomas J. 1990. "Embodiment as a Paradigm for Anthropology." *Ethos* 18 (1): 5–47.

Deering, David. 1996. Review of *Compassion Fatigue: Coping with Secondary Traumatic Stress Disorder in Those Who Treat the Traumatized*, edited by Charles R. Figley. *Journal of Psychosocial Nursing and Mental Health Services* 34 (11): 52.

de Waal, Frans. 2008. "Putting the Altruism Back into Altruism: The Evolution of Empathy." *Annual Review of Psychology* 59: 279–300.

Eisenberg, Nancy, and Janet Strayer. 1987. *Empathy and Its Development*. Cambridge Studies in Social and Emotional Development. Cambridge: Cambridge University Press.

Geertz, Clifford. 1975. "On the Nature of Anthropological Understanding: Not Extraordinary Empathy but Readily Observable Symbolic Forms Enable the Anthropologist to Grasp the Unarticulated Concepts that Inform the Lives and Cultures of Other Peoples." *American Scientist* 63 (1): 47–53.

———. 1984 (1976). "'From the Native's Point of View': On the Nature of Anthropological Understanding." In *Culture Theory*, ed. Richard A. Shweder and Robert A. LeVine, 123–136. Cambridge: Cambridge University Press.

Gelley, Alexander. 1999. "Contexts of the Aesthetic in Walter Benjamin." *Modern Language Notes* 114 (5): 933–61.

Gubar, Susan. 2002. "Empathic Identification in Anne Michaels's *Fugitive Pieces*: Masculinity and Poetry after Auschwitz." *Signs* 28 (1): 249–76.

Hirsch, Marianne. 2002. "Marked by Memory: Feminist Reflections on Trauma and Transmission." In *Extremities: Trauma, Testimony, and Community*, edited by Nancy K. Miller and Jason Tougaw, 71–91. Urbana: University of Illinois Press.

Hollan, Douglas, and C. Jason Throop. 2008. "Whatever Happened to Empathy?" *Ethos* 36 (4): 385–401.

Keen, Suzanne. 2006. "A Theory of Narrative Empathy." *Narrative* 14 (3): 207–36.

Kirmayer, Laurence J. 2008. "Empathy and Alterity in Cultural Psychiatry." *Ethos* 36 (4): 457–74.

Kohut, Heinz. 1959. "Introspection, Empathy, and Psychoanalysis: An Examination of the Relationship between Mode of Observation and Theory." *Journal of the American Psychoanalytic Association* 7: 459–83.

LaCapra, Dominick. 1999. "Trauma, Absence, Loss." *Critical Inquiry* 25 (4): 696–727.

Laub, Dori, and Nanette C. Auerhahn. 1989. "Failed Empathy—a Central Theme in the Survivor's Holocaust Experience." *Psychoanalytic Psychology* 6 (4): 377–400.

Lindahl, Carl. 2012. "Legends of Hurricane Katrina: The Right to Be Wrong, Survivor-to-Survivor Storytelling, and Healing." *Journal of American Folklore* 125 (496): 139–76.

Lipps, Theodore. 1979. "Empathy, Inner Imitation, and Sense Feelings." Translated by Melvin Rader and Max Schertel from *Archiv für die gesamte Psychologie* 1 (1903). In *A Modern Book of Aesthetics*, edited by Melvin M. Rader, 371–78. New York: Holt.

Mitchell, Michele, dir. 2015. *The Uncondemned*. Brooklyn: Film at Eleven Media.

Moyn, Samuel. 2006. "Empathy in History, Empathizing with Humanity." *History and Theory* 45 (3): 397–415.

Nowrojee, Binaifer. 1996. *Shattered Lives: Sexual Violence during the Rwandan Genocide and Its Aftermath*. New York: Human Rights Watch. https://www.hrw.org/report/1996/09/24/shattered-lives-sexual-violence-during-rwandan-genocide-and-its-aftermath.

Nussbaum, Emily. 2016. "Empathy for the Devil: Radical Loss on *Orange Is the New Black*." *New Yorker*, July 11 and 18, 2016, 86–87.

Ochs, Elinor, Tami Kremer-Sadlik, Karen Sirota, and Olga Solomon. 2004. "Autism and the Social World: An Anthropological Perspective." *Discourse Studies* 6 (2): 147–83.

Povinelli, Elizabeth A. 2001. "Radical Worlds: The Anthropology of Incommensurability and Inconceivability." *Annual Review of Anthropology* 30: 319–34.

Roemer, Michael. 1995. "The Rejection of Empathy." In *Telling Stories: Postmodernism and the Invalidation of Traditional Narrative*, 241–48. Lanham, MD: Rowman & Littlefield.

Shapiro, Joseph P. 1993. *No Pity: People with Disabilities Forging a New Civil Rights Movement*. New York: Three Rivers.

Shuman, Amy. 2005. *Other People's Stories: Entitlement Claims and the Critique of Empathy*. Urbana: University of Illinois Press.

———. 2006. "Entitlement and Empathy in Personal Narrative." *Narrative Inquiry* 16: 148–55.

Spector, Scott. 1998. "Edith Stein's Passing Gestures: Intimate Histories, Empathic Portraits." *New German Critique* 75: 28–56.

Stein, Edith. 1989. *On the Problem of Empathy*. Translated by Waltraut Stein. Vol. 3 of *The Collected Works of Edith Stein*. Washington, DC: ICS.

Amy SHUMAN is Professor in the Department of English at the Ohio State University. She is author of *Storytelling Rights: The Uses of Oral and Written Texts among Urban Adolescents* and *Other People's Stories: Entitlement Claims and the Critique of Empathy*. With Carol Bohmer, she is author of *Rejecting Refugees: Political Asylum in the 21st Century* and *Political Asylum Deceptions: The Culture of Suspicion*.

7

THE INTANGIBLE LIGHTNESS
OF HERITAGE

Michael Dylan Foster

I AM NEITHER A SURVIVOR NOR AN ETHNOGRAPHER of disaster. My observations are distant and filtered through mass media and secondhand accounts. But in this chapter, I begin with a brief personal narrative from my own fieldwork in Japan that has allowed me to imagine, ever so slightly, something about the ways people and communities can cope with the immeasurable sadness and irreversible changes of disaster and trauma.

For over a decade now, I have pursued fieldwork on a small island off the southwest coast of Kyushu. This is about as far away as you can get from the devastating Great East Japan Earthquake, the resulting tsunami, and the continuing nuclear catastrophe in the northeast of the main island of Honshu. Yet, somehow, in an indirect but poignant way, my relationship with people in that community far from the disaster site became a lens through which to consider the events of March 11, 2011—or simply "3.11" as it is often called in Japan. It is, of course, impossible for me to think from a survivor's perspective or even begin to identify with the experiences or feelings of people who have lived through these events. But by listening—even from a distance—and placing those narratives in a more familiar context, perhaps we can begin to make connections and participate in a dialogue about how to make sense of the senseless. For me, it was by contemplating my own experience of a "failed" ethnography against the unfolding devastation in Tohoku that I learned something about the meaning of tradition and how it can help individuals and groups persist in the face of otherwise unbearable loss. Perhaps too it is appropriate to begin with this personal narrative as a way of entering into the larger issues that disaster and trauma raise, because so often it is the act of storytelling that makes it possible to imagine distant events and the emotions of others.

My own research focuses on what, in recent years, has come to be termed "intangible cultural heritage," an awkward and bureaucratic phrase, to be sure, but one that encompasses a wide range of expressive cultural forms, including festivals, rituals, and other types of events. To deepen my own understanding of one such form, I have tried to spend as much time as possible in the community in which it takes place, something not easily done if that community happens to be in Japan and you happen to live in the United States. While we often talk of ethnography in terms of immersion in a culture different from the one in which we spend our daily lives, sometimes such immersion can be difficult, and fieldwork must be snatched in small bits and quick forays, as if gathering up crumbs with the hope of assembling the flavor of the whole.[1]

Fortunately, the particular form of intangible cultural heritage I have been studying is a ritual that takes place on New Year's Eve, which means I am on winter break from my job teaching at a university and can—if funding permits—travel to Japan for a few days. Such spotty visitation is far from perfect, but since I have worked in this particular site for so long now, even a few days of research can prove fruitful. After each little foray of this sort, I come away with a slightly deeper understanding of the ritual and the people who participate in it. Every visit is a discovery.

The ritual is formally known as *Koshikijima no Toshidon* and more casually called *Toshidon*.[2] It revolves around what Japanese folklorists often refer to as *raihōshin*, or "visiting deities," in which a community is visited once a year by frightening demon-deity figures from another world. In the case of Toshidon, the deities (who are also called Toshidon) descend from the "skyworld" on New Year's Eve. In practice, these Toshidon are community members, usually young men, who put on gigantic colorful masks made of painted cardboard and dress in costumes assembled from cloth, straw, and the fronds of local plants. In groups of five or six, they go from house to house, where they inquisition children, scolding them for bad behavior and praising them for their accomplishments throughout the preceding year. To the children, of course, these demonic figures are frightening; the experience is a test of bravery, often faced with tears and trembling voices, and just as often boasted about with family and friends the next day. The Toshidon only spend about twenty minutes in each household, but for the children it is a rite of passage they will always remember.

I am simplifying this, of course, because Toshidon takes place simultaneously in several different neighborhoods and each has its own set of procedures and protocols. Like any tradition, Toshidon has a long and complex history, and it changes incrementally from year to year depending on the participants and the needs of the moment—one reason I have tried to return as often as possible. I should also mention that in 2009 Toshidon was added to UNESCO's Representative List of the Intangible Cultural Heritage of Humanity. This was big news on the island, and it caused residents to deeply consider the broader theoretical questions of just what "intangible cultural heritage" means.[3]

Beyond this, the details of Toshidon are not critical to my essay, but I do want to stress the location: the island of Shimo-Koshikijima has approximately 1,700 households and is located twenty-five miles off the west coast of Kagoshima Prefecture in southwestern Japan. It is somewhat difficult to get to—especially when you are coming from the United States. And this is where my own narrative begins.

The Best Laid Plans

In 2010, both my partner and I were teaching at Indiana University. In the fall, we devised a plan for winter break that would allow us to meet various family responsibilities (mine in California, hers in Japan) and also give me a chance to visit Shimo-Koshikijima for Toshidon. Allowing some time for intensive end-of-semester grading, our schedule had us arriving in Japan on December 26. I would stay for a few days with my in-laws at their home near Yokohama and then travel by train to Satsumasendai in Kagoshima Prefecture, where I would spend one night and then take a ferry to Shimo-Koshikijima on the afternoon of the thirtieth. Even if something went awry and I was a day late, I could still take the ferry on the thirty-first and arrive in time for Toshidon that evening. Everything was in place: I contacted friends on the island, reserved train tickets and hotel rooms, and even booked my ferry tickets.

The first glitch occurred before we even arrived in California from Indiana. In brief, our plane was rerouted to an airport two hours from our destination; we were stranded in the rain; our luggage was lost for days; my partner caught a cold and was advised not to immediately fly. We managed to rebook our flight (losing hundreds of dollars), made an international connection with seconds to spare, and arrived in Narita to find the trains to Yokohama canceled. In the end, we finally did make it to my in-laws' house, but not until late in the evening of December 28, two days later than planned. I would need to leave early the next morning to travel down to the coast of Kagoshima Prefecture, where I could catch the ferry the next morning for the island. It had been a pretty terrible trip, but miraculously it looked as though I would still make it in time for Toshidon—and with a day to spare.

The next morning, hazy from jet lag, I boarded the bullet train, and by eight in the evening, I was in a cheap hotel in Satsumasendai. Excitedly, I called my friend Okazaki Takeshi on the island to let him know I would be there the next day. He told me that a rare winter storm had been forecast for the afternoon so I should be sure to take the early-morning ferry.[4]

At six thirty the next morning, I was on my way out the door when my cell phone rang. It was Okazaki calling to let me know the morning ferry had been canceled. "All right," I said cheerfully. "How about afternoon?"

"Canceled."

"And tomorrow?"

"The storm is supposed to get worse."

As you have guessed by now, I did not make it to the island that year. I got back on the bullet train and returned to my in-laws' home for a New Year's Eve that was pleasant, to be sure, but not quite what I had planned.

Searching for Meaning

Somehow the disappointment of not getting to the island that year was all the more poignant because of the struggles it took to *almost* get there. After a trip fraught with so many difficulties, why was I frustrated at the final step, only twenty-five miles and one short ferry ride from my destination? It was tempting to look for meaning or causality, to interpret these events as signs that might provide insight into past events or guidance for future behavior. Perhaps I was meant to stay on the mainland for some mysterious purpose to be revealed within the next few days? One island friend laughingly suggested that this was clearly a message that I should spend more time with my in-laws.

But of course it is presumptuous to imagine some sort of controlling intelligence causing a winter storm just to prevent *me* from crossing over to the island. In fact, I have been speaking as if I were the only one whose plans were changed. But the storm affected lives throughout the region in infinite ways: people slipped in the snow, appointments were missed, meetings canceled, shops closed. And on the island, dozens of people were forced to change their plans. The island does not have a high school, so teenagers attend schools on the mainland, staying in dorms and other accommodations. How many could not return to the island to visit their families for the holiday? Inversely, other people were stranded on the island. At least one friend of mine was prevented from traveling to the mainland to visit his relatives.

The cancellation also affected the performance of Toshidon itself. In his fifties now, Okazaki has become a behind-the-scenes leader, guiding less seasoned performers but not actually wearing the mask himself. But because of the storm, one of the younger participants was stranded on the mainland, so Okazaki had to take over for him. Even then, there were still too few performers of appropriate age, so the young assistant principal of the elementary school wore a mask as well. Not born on the island himself, he participated with care, wary of speaking in a different dialect and revealing his identity to his own students.

Recently one island neighborhood has tried to develop its version of Toshidon as a tourist attraction, inviting twenty tourists each year to witness the ritual. But like me, these would-be tourists were stranded on the mainland.[5] And in the few small hotels on the island, there were plenty of empty rooms (and lost revenue). In short, this simple storm was a major occurrence for the small community. The cancellation of the ferries for two days at this critical time of year had ramifications for families, for the tourist industry, for commerce, and for ritual.

And yet none of my friends on the island expressed anything more than a vague sense of disappointment. As one put it, "I was hoping we could drink with you tonight, but I guess we'll have to wait until next year." He then added casually that his son had been stranded on the mainland too, so he would have to wait to see him as well. The islanders took it all in stride; a change of plan like this, it seems, was simply not a big deal.

Such an attitude, of course, is necessary in a rural community where livelihoods are at the mercy of weather and other natural conditions. As with fishing people elsewhere in the world, for example, those who work on the island's small fishing boats determine where to go and what to catch by season and tides and weather. Several times in the past, I had arranged to go fishing with my friend Shirai and arrived at the crack of dawn, only to stand with him and look out at the whitecaps as we shook our heads. For me it was an experience missed; for Shirai, a day's income. Inversely, I have also visited his house on a clear night to find him unexpectedly away. Just off the coast I could see his boat, and about a dozen others, brightly lit against the black sea, fishing for squid.

It is a given that any fishing or agricultural village is controlled by the vicissitudes of the weather, or rather, that the activities of the day are determined through a *negotiation* with the weather. Seasoned fishing folk know just how much they can push their luck on a swelling sea, and skilled farmers might harvest just before a killing frost. In such an environment, it is only appropriate that rituals, festivals, and similar traditions are equally subject to improvisation.

The Weight of Tradition

A year earlier, in 2009, I *had* made it to the island. That year had been particularly important because Toshidon had just been inscribed on UNESCO's Representative List of the Intangible Cultural Heritage of Humanity. This was a momentous occurrence: a global cultural body had acknowledged this small ritual on a tiny island so distant from Paris and other major cities where UNESCO meetings are held. How would my friends react to this international acknowledgment of their tradition? How would it affect the way they conceive of "heritage"?

I discovered that most people were excited about the designation but also wary of its ramifications. They adamantly resisted the possibility that such outside notice would cause their tradition to become crystallized. Toshidon was a ritual for disciplining children, they maintained, and if there were no children on the island, then Toshidon would cease to exist. As the population of children on the island has decreased in recent years, the possibility of there being no children of appropriate age in the near future is very real.

Furthermore, I was told, Toshidon had never had fixed rules for clothing and behavior anyway; it was a flexible ad hoc process, an improvisational "happening" that changed by necessity every year. I am generalizing here, but this was the attitude of almost everybody I spoke with—be they farmers or fishers, government employees, the postmaster, ferryboat operators, politicians, or construction workers.

But there was one dissenting opinion. When I left the island that year, at the dawn of 2010, I sat on the ferry next to a man I had never met before. The man, whom I will call Yamaguchi, was in his early fifties but looked younger; he was short and tightly muscled, with a smooth, tanned face. When I told him I was researching Toshidon, he stated sharply, "I have something to say." He explained that he was from the island but had lived for years on the mainland, raising his family and working various jobs. He told me he did not like the attention Toshidon was starting to get from the media. He believed the tradition had been corrupted in recent years. He was afraid it would become a spectacle and lose its meaning. He said the people in the village office, and my friends who had come to see me off when I boarded the ferry, didn't know a thing about Toshidon. Repeatedly, in his criticisms, he invoked a word that struck me as somewhat odd: *karui*, or "light." He told me that the people currently involved with Toshidon are *light*, the implication being that they take things *lightly*, that their knowledge is *light*, and that they are therefore making the tradition *light*.

It was a pretty rough ferry ride, in part because of a choppy sea but mainly because of Yamaguchi's criticisms. When we arrived, Yamaguchi gave me a lift to the train station, and I promised him I would think about what he had said.

And I have. Particularly the following year, after my failed attempt to get to the island, the notion of *lightness* began to take on a profundity I suspect Yamaguchi had not intended. When I realized I wasn't going to make it to the island, a heaviness washed over me. Events took on gravity; not only would I miss Toshidon but there seemed some weighty reason for having traveled so far only to be denied the chance. And yet, when I spoke with Okazaki, when I spoke with Shirai, they laughed it off. These things happen. They took the whole thing *lightly*.

And that is exactly the point. Yamaguchi was right: my friends on the island, the people who live with Toshidon, do take their tradition lightly, because it is only through this lightness of attitude that Toshidon retains flexibility through the capriciousness of weather and unforeseen circumstances. If tradition is too heavy, tradition bearers cannot sustain it. But if they hold it lightly, lifting it with grace and agility, the sort of delicate touch that allows for play and movement and tactical adjustment to circumstances, then there is always next year. Because of course, as folklorists have long known, any tradition, any sense of heritage, is predicated as much on the belief in continuity with the past and the future as it is on meaning in the present.

My failed ethnography had, ironically, turned into a very productive experience. By not making it to the island, I had learned a great deal about how the islanders apprehend the world and consider their activities within it. And this notion of lightness has become for me a touchstone for accessing the way people sustain their heritage. I fancy it a kind of intangible lightness: not something measurable or quantifiable, but a sort of intuition or skill like walking a tightrope, an ability to respond to the subtlest of changes. This is, not surprisingly, the very same kind of sensitivity and flexibility that allows a fishing or agricultural community to survive through times of storm or drought or other unpredictable circumstances. Every plan is always necessarily only *for now*. Heritage floats. I began pondering these ideas further and writing about this failed-but-therefore-successful ethnographic experience.

Infrastructures

But then, one morning in March 2011, I woke up in my Indiana home to news of the Tohoku earthquake, the tsunami, and the nuclear catastrophe. My friends on the island, safely ensconced in the southwest corner of Japan, were far from the epicenter. I knew they were safe. And yet, as I stared at the images streaming across my computer screen, I could not help but think of them. I watched and I read about how people in small communities— places like Kesennuma, Rikuzentakata, Ishinomaki—were coping, or trying to cope. And I imagined how the small community I know best, Shimo-Koshikijima, might deal with a similar situation.

Several weeks after the earthquake, I also began to wonder what happens to rituals, festivals, and similar activities in such devastating circumstances. If tradition and heritage, whether from an emic or an etic perspective, presume continuity between past, present, and future, what happens when the festival site has been wiped from the face of the land? What happens to a ritual for safe waters and a good catch, for example, when there is no longer a port, there are no longer any fishing boats, and the families that once operated them are dead? At times like this, does heritage become a frivolous luxury of a lost, happier world?

A picture in the *New Yorker* showed a flattened wasteland that was once Minami-Sanriku in Miyagi Prefecture. The caption read: "When the tsunami receded, some of the towns in a region that traced its history to the seventh century had ceased to exist in visible form" (Osnos 2011, 80–81).

In *visible form*. Does the heritage of a people or community have to be expressed through visible form? Is intangible heritage meaningless when the immediate concerns are tangible, like food and shelter?

I don't know the answers to these questions. But I wonder if it isn't exactly at that terrible moment when visible manifestations of heritage like ritual and festival seem irrelevant that the *intangible* meaning of the concept emerges. In the weeks and months after March 11, the Japanese were noted for their resilience, for the orderly way they coped with personal and national tragedy. I am by no means suggesting any sort of unique Japanese resiliency, but it seems that, at least in some communities, there was already in place a long and well-rehearsed set of human relationships—a command structure, as it were—that transcended even the loss of individual community members.

Less than two weeks after the disaster, a newspaper article about the hamlet of Hadenya in the Minami-Sanriku area explained that "the colossal wave that swept away this tiny fishing hamlet also washed out nearby bridges, phone lines and cellphone service, leaving survivors shivering and dazed and completely cut off at a hilltop community center" (Fackler 2011). Within days, however, despite the destruction of the technological and civic infrastructure, the villagers had created a governing body and a clinic, and they were systematically dividing up daily tasks such as finding fuel and preparing meals. When asked how all this was possible under such extreme circumstances, one of the leaders, Abe Osamu, explained that they "found it easy to cooperate because they had organized themselves to hold the village's religious festivals" (Fackler 2011). In other words, they already had in place the necessary structure of command, relationships, and cooperative experiences that made it possible for them to respond quickly and effectively to an unthinkable situation. Even though the tangible infrastructure of the community was literally washed away, the intangible infrastructure still held.

Perhaps I am extrapolating too broadly from this limited example—and certainly extended and varied fieldwork would be necessary to make an empirically valid point. Nor do I want to wax utopic or overly optimistic; years later, Hadenya, like so many other places devastated by the tragedy, is still struggling. But I would suggest that here we see heritage in practice—that is, heritage as a structure of leadership and responsibility. And at the same time, more profoundly, we also see the deeper role heritage plays in the lives of community residents. It provides, in essence, an *infrastructure of caring*: a template for working together that may normally be expressed through the performance of a given ritual or event but that can also be mobilized, in times of need, for organizing a shelter for survivors. Of such spontaneously organized groups, the mayor of Minami-Sanriku, Sato Jin, commented, "They are like extended families. . . . They provide support and comfort" (quoted in Fackler 2011).

I use the word *infrastructure* here intentionally because it reminds us that below what we see or experience, there are often taken-for-granted ways of interacting and operating that inform the structure of any community. "Good infrastructure is by definition invisible," explain Martha Lampland and Susan Leigh Star (2009, 17). It is "part of the background for other kinds of work." In its everyday sense, then, infrastructure is "something that other things 'run on,' things that are substrate to events and movements" (17). In my own research on Toshidon, for example, I have explored how the ritual event—the twenty minutes a year in which the demon-deities appear in the household—is supported by an infrastructure of shared understandings, relationships, hierarchies, and stories told by parents to their children. There is an invisible substrate that exists all year round and makes possible the visible New Year's Eve event. The ritual as it plays out on that single evening is only a superstructure, the tip of the iceberg, as it were, an above-the-surface projection of an unseen support system.

In the case of Hadenya, the particular event—the "religious festival"— may have been (temporarily) made meaningless by the disaster, but the infrastructure remained in place, this time supporting the creation of a temporary government and a clinic and an effective division of labor, all in the interest of survival. The very real system of human connections, of years of communication and working together in festivals and community events, allowed a community to organize itself effectively and efficiently in an evacuation center during a catastrophe. If heritage is "a mode of cultural production in the present that has recourse to the past" (Kirshenblatt-Gimblett 1995, 369), in certain circumstances such "cultural production" is not commodifiable, not appropriate for exhibition, not even visible. But it saves lives.

Again, I am wary of being too optimistic here. Infrastructures are built through human relations, and human relations are inflected with the faults and shortsightedness and biases of any society and the specific individuals who constitute it. Rural Japanese communities are certainly not immune to discrimination and intolerance. Historical hierarchies and local prejudices are often reflected in the performance of rituals and festivals and may also be reflected in the emergency superstructures created after a catastrophe. My point here is to suggest that the existence of active, living traditions within a community, of this intangible thing called cultural heritage, simply means that there is already an infrastructure on which a superstructure of support can be built in the first place.[6]

Subject to Change

In Hadenya, the superstructural artifact that runs on the infrastructure comprised the practical systems of governance, health care, and labor that were constructed after evacuation. We might say that the artifact of the "tradition" itself was replaced completely by a temporary set of institutions that were much more relevant to the situation at hand. In a sense, this is a purely instrumental use of the infrastructure of caring that survived the cataclysm.

But even while communities were mobilizing their infrastructures for such practical and explicitly caregiving purposes, many communities made an express point of also continuing to perform their festivals and traditions within the context of post-disaster recovery. Perhaps the very act of running something on the infrastructure can itself help energize the community and perpetuate the human relations that constitute it. A quick perusal of newspaper reports that appeared in the weeks and months after March 11 reveals a fierce determination that "celebrations" should persist despite—or because of—the adversity of the situation. At first glance, such persistence might seem almost a willful denial of the depth of the tragedy, but clearly there is something more going on here.[7] Less than a month after the disaster, for example, mayors from three cities in Tohoku, worried about "a national mood of self-restraint," announced that they would proceed with their summer festivals because they "wanted to project the vitality of the Tohoku region" (*Asahi shinbun* 2011b). If we think of this in terms of narrative, we are in a sense watching the characters hijack the story, assuming agency in their own tale to create a narrative they want to share with others.

In the city of Morioka, it was announced that Morioka Sansa-Odori, a major summer festival, would be held as usual but with certain modifications: the annual Miss Sansa-Odori Contest would not be open to the public, and because of energy shortages, the time of the parade would be adjusted according to the availability of electricity; moreover, electrical generators would be prepared (*Asahi shinbun* 2011c). To be sure, the summer festivals here are large city events, and their continued production was as much a way to encourage a return of tourism as it was to provide residents a sense of continuity with the past and hope for normalcy in the future. But I want to stress here the attitude of lightness with which leaders and residents approached their heritage, their willingness to modify or reinvent tradition to accommodate the needs of a community in crisis.

Even more striking, however, is the persistence of festival production within smaller, tighter communities, where infrastructure was engaged for the residents alone. In this context, the very performance of tradition in the face of diversity becomes both a sign of, and a catalyst for, community vitality. If the residents are creating their own narrative here, it is one that they tell themselves *for* themselves.

On April 24, only six weeks after the catastrophe, for example, the residents of Kamaishi City in Iwate Prefecture joined together to perform a tiger dance (*tora-mai*) traditionally enacted as a prayer for safety at sea. Some twenty group members played drums and danced. Over half of these participants had lost their homes in the tsunami, and two group members had been killed. The remaining members had struggled over whether it was appropriate to perform so soon after the tragedy but eventually determined that their performance "would give strength to the citizens." Watching at the evacuation center, one woman said, "Even through all this, they have come." Another said, "It makes me cry" (*Asahi shinbun* 2011d). The performance itself articulates a story of revitalization and strength, and it acts, in a sense, as a sort of self-fulfilling prophecy or speech act—its very telling makes the story true and changes the reality of the situation.

In May 2011, more than half the residents of the Kugunari-hama district in Ishinomaki City (Miyagi Prefecture) were still living in evacuation centers. Most homes had been washed away; four people were dead; one was still missing. When time came for the spring festival (*matsuri*), some residents wondered whether it was really appropriate. But sixty-three-year-old Numakura Keiichi argued, "I want to have a festival to pray for recovery." He enlisted other residents and the priest of the shrine, and they decided to go ahead. Although the main building of the shrine itself was intact, the *torii* gate had been washed away and the area was littered with debris; they cleared it away with heavy machinery, and on May 3, over one hundred people gathered for the festival. "It has been a long time since we saw cheerful faces," said one participant (*Asahi shinbun* 2011e).

And one more powerful example—this one from the Ōishi district of Rikuzen-Takata City in Iwate Prefecture. The district had been devastated: of 160 households, only 40 remained; of 350 residents, 80 were still missing. Yet on March 23, only twelve days after the catastrophe, residents performed their local tiger dance. In front of the once-submerged community center, on a landscape littered with upside-down fire trucks and the remains of destroyed homes, they danced wildly with glimmering black masks and "black and yellow striped cloth waving this way and that." The dance, as the *Asahi shinbun* newspaper points out, was "originally" a custom in which the dancers would go from house to house ritualistically exorcising bad fortune on the "little New Year holiday" (*koshōgatsu*), around January 15. Here then, on a different date and in a different location, the existing infrastructure and know-how were deployed to create a performance with a different (or perhaps eerily similar) function and narrative. "Just being at the evacuation center makes you depressed," explained Satō Minoru, one of the dancers. "We cannot let our protective deity (*mamori-gami*) sleep beneath the wreckage" (*Asahi shinbun* 2011a).

Judging from this sampling of newspaper articles, it seems that in the weeks immediately following the catastrophe, as one reporter observed, "the traditions and beliefs of Tohoku have become a form of spiritual support for the victims" (*Asahi shinbun* 2011a). Moreover, in many cases the need to preserve and give new life to tradition functioned to hold the fabric of the community together. In the words of a seventy-five-year-old Ōishi woman who was working with younger residents to reconstruct items used in a summer festival: "So much has been washed away. I want to make sure the community bonds (*kizuna*) still remain" (*Asahi shinbun* 2011a).

I don't want to extrapolate too much from this very limited and anecdotal material.[8] To a large degree, such newspaper articles reveal as much about the media spin and the hopes of readers watching from a distance as they do about the on-the-ground sentiments of people struggling to survive. Media reports like this tend to be too neat, to affirm too easily the dominant narrative of a hopeful portrayal of resistance, revitalization, and triumph.[9] Years after the earthquake and tsunami, life in affected areas is anything but "normal." The dead and missing are not forgotten; businesses have yet to recover; many residents have not been able to return home; others have moved to other parts of the country where they are struggling to rebuild their lives and livelihoods. And the unabated, slow-motion disaster that is the Fukushima Daiichi Nuclear Power Plant has continued to play out tragically against the bumbling excuses of the Tokyo Electric Power Company and the criminal hypocrisies of the Japanese government.

But my point is neither a political one nor an essentialist argument for the resilience of the Japanese spirit—or even, for that matter, the resilience of the human spirit. Rather, I simply want to observe that, even in the depths of unimaginable loss, some value can be squeezed from this thing scholars call heritage. On the one hand, it provides a sense of continuity, a linking of the present with the past and with a desire to persist into the future. Soon after the disaster, a sixty-six-year-old carpenter in Ōishi began fixing the accoutrements for the local *Tanabata* festival. "Even after ten years, I don't think we will be able to perform our festival," he explained to a reporter. "But if we [remake everything] little by little, the festival will be revived by the time of my grandchildren or great-grandchildren" (*Asahi shinbun* 2011a).

On the other hand, the existence of traditions within a given community also, as I have suggested, means that a set of relationships and operational practices are already in place. Such an infrastructure, of course, differs from community to community, but it is the thing that makes the performance of the tradition run smoothly every year. And it is also the thing that, as in Hadenya, kicks in when a festival or other event is the last thing on the minds of the residents.

But what I most want to stress here is that, despite the persistence of this infrastructure and despite the desire for the persistence of tradition itself, flexibility and willingness to change are key to actual practice. I have loosely invoked the notion of storytelling to suggest the way in which community members take command of their own stories to create a narrative that can inspire survival and recovery. To push the metaphor even further, we might think of infrastructure itself as a sort of tale type, providing a foundation on which a storyteller builds a narrative. And skilled storytellers, of course, are characterized by their flexibility and ability to improvise; the infrastructure of heritage allows residents to create their own stories through ritual and celebration, when words may not suffice. Whether it is the performance of a tiger dance in a different place and at a different time or the decision to cancel the Miss Sansa-Odori Contest, tradition is characterized by a light touch: flexibility, improvisation, and a willingness to negotiate with current realities. When those current realities are of devastation, then flexibility may entail extreme change, such as creating an evacuation center: a practical, life-giving facility that is as much a part of heritage as any festival or ritual dance.

Bearable Lightness

To return now to my own tale of failed ethnography with which I began, I hesitate to compare one of the most devastating natural disasters in history to a simple snowstorm that caused a ferry cancellation, but in a strange way it feels as if there is a connection between the idea that heritage is something to be taken lightly and the flexibility necessary to survive these extreme conditions. My friends in Shimo-Koshikijima accommodated changing circumstances with grace. Toshidon, as several islanders have explained to me, is nothing more than a metaphor, an articulation of the community's collective care for its members. The capriciousness of the weather shifted their procedures that year, slightly altering the metaphor, but did not fundamentally lessen its meaning and importance or damage the infrastructure on which it runs.

Through my own engagement with this one ritual, I can begin to imagine the complex role of heritage and its bearers in the communities affected by the catastrophe of March 11. The thing we call intangible cultural heritage is real and meaningful, but most importantly it is light—it *must* be light—because it is carried, from one year to the next, despite, and sometimes because of, unforeseeable occurrences. In the best of times, heritage may seem unbearably light, unsustainably light, but in the worst of times, it can bear people aloft.

Coda

I began this chapter by stressing the geographical distance between the site where the terrible events of March 11 occurred and the island of Shimo-Koshikijima, where Toshidon is performed. Despite that distance, my personal experiences with the island community made it possible for me to place March 11 into a somewhat familiar context and imagine how my own friends might cope with a similar situation. Ultimately, though, my ruminations remain only theoretical—a sort of imagined, intellectual effort at empathy, and an attempt to transcend difference both geographical and experiential. But given my stress on distance, ironically I was recently reminded of the very real connections between people and places, and of the inescapable interconnectedness of events, in a way that brought March 11 a little closer to the island I know so well. On August 11, 2015, the Kyushu Electric Power Company restarted one of its nuclear reactors—the first reactor to go online in Japan since the Fukushima disaster, after which all reactors in the country were shut down. That first reactor is at the Sendai Nuclear Power Plant, on the coast of Kagoshima Prefecture in the city of Satsumasendai—the municipality in which Shimo-Koshikijima is located. My friends on the island live only about thirty miles away.

Afterword, Added in 2021

In the coda above, I note that the first nuclear reactor was restarted in 2015. Now, over a decade since the 2011 disaster, there are nine reactors in operation at five separate power plants in Japan. In the Tohoku area, where the earthquake was centered, massive challenges remain. Tens of thousands of survivors have not returned. Two hundred eighty billion dollars have been invested in reconstructing the physical environment, but very little has been spent "in helping people to rebuild their lives by, for instance, offering mental health services for trauma" (Yamaguchi and Nuga 2021).

During the COVID-19 pandemic, I watched Japan from afar, curious and fearful as to how people would retain their festivals—characterized as they are by people coming together to perform, eat, and celebrate in ways that have always transcended "social distancing." For the most part, I think, communities have responded with flexibility, with some events canceled outright and others downsized or creatively modified. At least from my distant view, people seemed to react with agility, holding onto their traditions lightly—allowing them to remain afloat for better times.

In contrast, the Japanese government was weighed down by a desire to produce its own festival for global consumption: the Summer Olympic Games. Cancelled in 2020, these had been rescheduled for the summer of 2021, at which time officials were determined to proceed with their plans despite a vexingly slow vaccine rollout, warnings of viral spread, and a majority of citizens arguing for postponement or another cancellation. For a variety of reasons—entrenched nationalism, commercial self-interest—neither the Japanese government nor the International Olympic Committee responded to the moment with the combination of flexibility and care we have seen in smaller community settings. To be sure, in the end, both the Olympics and Paralympics did proceed (devoid of spectators)—but this occurred amidst an upsurge of COVID cases in Japan described by experts at the time as "a disaster-level emergency situation that is out of control" (*Nikkei Asia* 2021).

The pandemic has, of course, produced unparalleled challenges worldwide—Japan is no exception—with every community struggling to respond appropriately not only to the disease itself but also to the ruptures it brought about in social interaction and cultural activity. As the immediate crisis of COVID starts to fade into history, I am excited to watch the return of local festivals and other forms of intangible cultural heritage. I suspect that those which people held onto lightly will emerge from the breach with renewed vigor and dynamism. They will continue to tell the stories they have always told, of values and history and beliefs, but there will also be fresh elements to their performance, innovations born of experience and survival, providing new layers of meaning in an ongoing narrative.

Notes

1. Recently, scholars have actively started to theorize this sort of engagement with a community, which they broadly label "patchwork ethnography." See Günel, Varma, and Watanabe (2020).

2. "Koshikijima no Toshidon" literally means "Toshidon of the Koshiki Islands" and is the name under which the ritual was recorded as an "important intangible folk cultural property" (*jūyō mukei minzoku bunkazai*) with the Japanese Agency for Cultural Affairs in 1977. This is also the name as it was inscribed on UNESCO's Representative List of the Intangible Cultural Heritage of Humanity in 2009 (also 2018). On the island, however, it is generally just called "Toshidon."

3. There are a number of rituals similar to Toshidon practiced elsewhere in Japan; Toshidon is also not unlike mumming and other practices in various cultures throughout the world. My description here is based primarily on Toshidon in the communities of Motomachi and Fumoto. For more on Toshidon and UNESCO, see Foster (2011, 2013, 2015). I have been researching Toshidon since 1999 and have observed the ritual in 1999, 2000, 2009, 2011, 2012, and 2016; I have also conducted fieldwork on Shimo-Koshikijima at other times of the year and lived full-time on the island from December 2011 to May 2012. I want to express my endless gratitude to my many friends on the island who have welcomed me warmly into their community and generously shared with me their thoughts on Toshidon—and so much more.

4. All names of islanders are pseudonyms.

5. The following year (2011), I had the opportunity to meet several of the tourists who had been stranded, and all of them of course had their own stories to tell about the experience.

6. In a contrasting case in the United States, sisters Caitria and Morgan O'Neill have discussed their own experience of a tornado in their hometown of Monson, Massachusetts, and the difficulties they faced because of a lack of infrastructure: "During a painful period, our community learned how to manage volunteers and donations, track data, apply for grants and request aid through official channels. We bumbled through the early days, doing things wrong and wasting time. Eventually a system emerged, coordinated largely by the First Church of Monson and a few dedicated local volunteers. But why did we have to

build that system on our own? Though we were prepared to survive the storm, why hadn't someone prepared us for recovery?" (O'Neill 2012). The sisters' experience of creating "a functional infrastructure for recovery" inspired them to found Recover.org, which they call "the idealization of the infrastructure they built: a clean, easy-to-use recovery software framework that can be deployed before a disaster to prepare communities" (see "Recovers: Community-Powered Disaster Recovery" [blog], accessed April 10, 2022, https://recovers .wordpress.com/about/).

7. For one detailed example after another earthquake, see chap. 2.

8. Of course, fieldwork with affected people would certainly reveal more nuanced information and details. But in part because of the onslaught of researchers into the disaster areas, as documented in chap. 2, I am hesitant myself to intrude into communities where I have no long-standing relationship. My point rather is that even by observing from a distance, we can learn to better understand the communities with which we do have connections.

9. For an insightful critique of such media-controlled dominant narratives in the case of Hurricane Katrina, see chap. 5. See also Shuman's work on empathy, in chap. 6 of this book and elsewhere, for insight into questions of distance.

References

Asahi shinbun. 2011a. "Dentō, tashikana kizuna, oreramo nando demo tachiagaru shika-neebe: Tora-mai, goshinboku, kōdai shūraku." March 26, 2011, evening edition, 12.

———. 2011b. "Tōhoko 3-shi: 'Matsuri shitai.'" April 8, 2011, Tokyo morning edition, 4.

———. 2011c. "Morioka sansa-odori, 8-gatsu kaisai kimaru." April 16, 2011, Iwate Prefecture morning edition, 25.

———. 2011d. "Shimin o genki-zuke: Dentō no tora-mai hirō." April 25, 2011, Iwate Prefecture morning edition, 15.

———. 2011e. "Dakara koso rei taisai: Ishinomaki, Kugunarihama, fukkō negai kaisai." May 4, 2011, Miyagi Prefecture morning edition, 17.

Fackler, Martin. 2011. "Severed From the World, Villagers Survive on Tight Bonds and To-Do Lists." *New York Times*, March 23, 2011. https://www.nytimes.com/2011/03/24/world /asia/24isolated.html?searchResultPosition=2.

Foster, Michael Dylan. 2011. "The UNESCO Effect: Confidence, Defamiliarization, and a New Element in the Discourse on a Japanese Island." *Journal of Folklore Research* 48 (1): 63–107.

———. 2013. "Shikakuteki sōzō: 'Koshikijima no Toshidon' ni okeru miru/mirareru kankei no ichi kōsatsu." *Nihon minzokugaku* 273 (February): 55–95.

———. 2015. "UNESCO on the Ground." *Journal of Folklore Research* 52 (2–3): 143–56.

Günel, Gökçe, Saiba Varma, and Chika Watanabe. 2020. "A Manifesto for Patchwork Ethnography." Member Voices, *Fieldsights*, June 9. https://culanth.org/fieldsights/a -manifesto-for-patchwork-ethnography.

Kirshenblatt-Gimblett, Barbara. 1995. "Theorizing Heritage." *Ethnomusicology* 39 (3): 367–80.

Lampland, Martha, and Susan Leigh Star, eds. 2009. *Standards and Their Stories: How Quantifying, Classifying, and Formalizing Practices Shape Everyday Life.* Ithaca, NY: Cornell University Press.

Nikkei Asia. 2021. "Disease Experts Seek Halving of Tokyo Foot Traffic to Curb COVID."
August 12, 2021. https://asia.nikkei.com/Spotlight/Coronavirus/Disease-experts-seek
-halving-of-Tokyo-foot-traffic-to-curb-COVID.

O'Neill, Caitria. 2012. "How Communities Bounce Back from Disaster." CNN, September 2,
2012. http://edition.cnn.com/2012/09/02/opinion/oneill-disaster-recovery/index.html.

Osnos, Evan. 2011. "Aftershocks: A Nation Bears the Unbearable." *New Yorker,* March 28, 2011.

Yamaguchi, Mari, and Haruka Nuga. 2021. "'At the Starting Line Again': Survivors Still
Struggle to Recover from 2011 Quake, Tsunami." *Los Angeles Times,* March 9, 2021.
https://www.latimes.com/world-nation/story/2021-03-09/residents-struggling-recover
-decade-after-fukushima-earthquake-tsunami.

Michael Dylan FOSTER is Professor in the Department of East Asian Languages and Cultures at the University of California, Davis. His books include *The Book of Yōkai: Mysterious Creatures of Japanese Folklore* (2015) and the coedited volume *UNESCO on the Ground: Local Perspectives on Intangible Cultural Heritage* (Indiana University Press, 2015).

8

DOCUMENTING DISASTER FOLKLORE IN THE EYE OF THE STORM

Six Months after María

Gloria M. Colom Braña

THIS CHAPTER IS BASED ON A BLOG SERIES written for Indiana University's Diverse Environmentalisms Research Team between six and eight months after Hurricane María made landfall in Puerto Rico on September 20, 2017. Using my experiences as a graduate student in the field of folklore conducting ethnographic fieldwork for my dissertation in Arecibo, Puerto Rico, I focus on the use of traditional knowledge and innovation for survival in times of disaster. Writing this piece has become part of the healing process for coping with and understanding the effects of the hurricane on my life, research, family, and community, as well as on the island where I was born and raised.

Before

Has it already been half a year since Hurricane María? Sometimes it feels like decades. Sometimes it feels like only a few days.

As I sit at my computer in Bloomington, Indiana, I am constantly aware of the passage of time, of continuing news of power outages, of people who still live without home security, job security, or even knowledge of whether they will eat tomorrow. The six-month benchmark is also the first time I can finally sit down and, without freezing or panicking, write about documenting folk knowledge as it was applied within the context of a natural disaster. Reading Ruth Behar's (1996) book *The Vulnerable Observer*, about the vulnerability of exposing one's own participation in ethnographic documentation, has helped me process the flowing boundary between lived experience, identity as a community member, and trauma.

My husband, Miguel A. Cruz Díaz, and I have been working toward our doctorates in history and folklore, respectively, over the last four years at Indiana University. We both completed our qualifying exams and defended our proposals by spring of 2017 and decided to take advantage of the summer and fall to do dissertation research. Our plan was to spend a few weeks in Amsterdam, where Miguel was conducting archival research, and then travel to Puerto Rico. Miguel would stay with me there for several weeks before returning to Indiana. I would remain in Puerto Rico for an additional four months, from July to October, doing ethnographic fieldwork and site documentation for my dissertation on traditional uses of domestic spaces. The plan called for documenting houses and their *marquesinas* (carports) in the city of Arecibo, on the northern coast of the island, where I would stay with my in-laws Miguel Sr. and Carmen. On the weekends I would visit my mother and brothers in Aguadilla, about fifty minutes away.

Having grown up in Puerto Rico, I knew not only that my stay on the island would coincide with the six-month hurricane season but that I would be there during its peak between August and October. The most intense period in the season is mid-September, when most hurricanes and tropical storms land on Puerto Rico (Boose, Serrano, and Foster 2004, 342). Nonetheless, hurricanes are an accepted eventuality for people living in the Caribbean—along with earthquakes, tsunamis, flash floods, and droughts.

Foreshadowing?

The first person I interviewed on this trip was my own grandfather, Francisco Braña Nieves (known fondly by his grandchildren as Abuelito Cico). Ninety years old at the time of the interview, he was clear of mind and renowned for his cutting wit and strong character. When asked about his youth, Abuelito described his house in the mountains of Bayamón during the 1930s. However, the conversation quickly changed from architecture to his first powerful memory. He told me about experiencing Hurricane San Ciprián in 1932, when he was five years old, explaining how the house survived the storm because of the strength of its hardwood columns. Even with this strength, staying in the house during the hurricane was never an option. Abuelito considered the house stronger than most of the neighboring

MARQUESINA

Fig. 8.1. A typical house made with a combination of poured concrete and reinforced concrete blocks with a flat roof and *marquesina* (carport).

bohíos, the traditional wood or thatch-and-palm houses that were home to over 80 percent of the population at the time, but when the hurricane came, his family took shelter in the *barraca* (barracks), also called the *tormentera* (storm shelter), which was carefully maintained for the eventuality of a storm. The tormentera, a low-lying triangular structure often built partially underground, was generally made of the same renewable and organic materials as the bohío but had a geometric design that allowed for the aerodynamic flow of air over the building, protecting those inside.

In 1932, storm-tracking technology was still in its infancy. People living in rural Puerto Rico relied mainly on knowledge of the land and subtle changes in the weather to recognize the signs of an incoming storm so they could reach the closest tormentera before the gales began. The saying "Red sky at night, sailor's delight. Red sky in morning, sailor's warning" has variants in sources as old as the Bible and has been used on both land and sea to forecast weather (Science Reference Section 2019). I remember my father telling me as I was growing up that before a hurricane the sky sometimes becomes red. I had only witnessed this once, early one morning before an unnamed cyclonic formation. I still remember the sky, landscape, trees, and house tinting red for a few minutes before the sky turned slate gray. My grandfather and great-grandparents would have looked for similar cues in the sky along with subtler signs, such as the leaves becoming very still and the air hot and heavy.

BARRACA | TORMENTERA

Fig. 8.2. Traditional *barraca* or *tormentera* used as a storm shelter.

For Abuelito's family, the telltale sign was the sky turning lead gray with smaller light-gray clouds dashing underneath. If it was indeed a hurricane rather than a tropical wave or storm, a strong gust of wind lasting between two and ten minutes would turn the leaves upside down, formally announcing the quickly approaching storm. After the first gust, there might be a few minutes or a few hours before the high winds picked up. It was imperative to reach safety and secure the family and neighbors as soon as possible. Abuelito also mentioned other sensory clues, such as the smell of brine and fish miles inland, and he described looking out for *el ojo del buey*, literally "the bull's eye," the larger circular movement of ponderous clouds.

When San Ciprián struck Puerto Rico, Abuelito recalled, there was nothing to do but wait and literally hold tight. The men held on to the central beam, either with their hands or by pulling down on ropes during the peak of the storm, as gales tried to pull the roof upward. After the storm, almost a full day later, the family emerged from the tormentera to find crops and homes destroyed and a long slow reconstruction process awaiting them. The rice crop had been flattened but was somewhat salvageable, as were many of the tubers such as yams and cassava, whose roots were protected underground.

My grandfather gave me this detailed account of a hurricane that had torn through the island eighty-five years earlier right at the beginning of the 2017 peak hurricane season. Even during the interview, the irony of the timing was not lost on me, but like everybody who lives in a hurricane zone, I considered this just one more thing to be factored into the daily reality.

I concentrated on my dissertation research and hoped for the best.

Storms on the Horizon

The season was beginning to pick up in mid-August. I was glued to my phone wondering whether my extended family in Houston was safe as Hurricane Harvey became stationary over the city. As reports came of rising water, I would check in every few hours to ask my mother whether family members had been in contact yet. I also frequently checked the National Oceanic and Atmospheric Administration maps of the Atlantic Ocean to see what was developing off the coast of Africa.

I was in Arecibo in early September when Hurricane Irma began developing quickly, with increasingly nightmarish wind speeds. The trajectory sent it near enough to Puerto Rico that any shift southward would prove catastrophic. My youngest brother called and asked if I could help with storm preparations at home. An hour later we were on our way to Aguadilla, recounting the checklist we already knew by heart. Did we have enough canned foods, batteries, candles, flashlights, bottles of water? Were the battered old radio and the landline phone still working? Could we secure the large glass windows?

The next day the sky was slate gray, with low-lying clouds speeding by underneath. But the weather services gave us more than twelve hours before any real danger, so we went ahead and secured all that we could, storing any loose patio furniture. We also harvested as many fruits as possible, such as *quenepas* (a locally grown fruit), still-too-young papayas, coconuts, and far too many avocados. An abundance of avocados in particular was said to be a portent of storms, in part because avocado season in Puerto Rico coincides with peak hurricane season and in part because the association has been repeated so many times as folk knowledge by our elders that it has become accepted as fact. That September, there were so many avocados we sometimes ate them three times a day.

None of the hurricane-forecasting models predicted landfall on the western coast of Puerto Rico, so our plan was to mitigate damage rather than board up the whole house. We decluttered the bedrooms, covered beds in plastic, and relocated to the living room and Mom's bedroom to wait

Fig. 8.3. Supplies and the mental checklist.

with the radio. In the end, Irma, the strongest Category 5 that I could recall, decimated many neighboring islands and did considerable damage to the towns of eastern Puerto Rico. But the rest of the island was spared.

The storm, however, became a stress test of the already fragile infrastructure. With the first gust of wind, the electricity failed, and soon afterward, we lost water and phone services. By the next day, most of the island was still without electricity, and many people would not regain power for over a year. If a storm that barely grazed us could obliterate these structures, what would a direct hit bring? With this new unease, I continued to refresh the Atlantic Ocean maps at least once a day. Mid-September was fast approaching, and there were too many huge clouds for my liking.

María

September 17 in Arecibo was a lovely if extremely hot day, with a humidity index above 110 degrees Fahrenheit. My field notes say, "Another hurricane is coming—this one is of normal scale, but it is going to flatten us. The internet

Fig. 8.4. Although most concrete houses are designed to resist hurricane winds, windows are usually boarded up to avoid severe damage within the house.

jokes and memes have commenced—it is called María, and José is still circling around. We have had devastating hurricane years, but I don't remember so many coming so quickly."[1] Ada Monzón, a Puerto Rican meteorologist who gained an almost cultlike following because of her accurate if terrifying updates on Hurricane Irma, was now comparing the American and European prediction models. Both showed María coming in through the south, a trajectory considered more dangerous than a northern path. One model predicted a tropical storm and the other a Category 5, but both sent it on a path that crossed the full island around Thursday, September 21.

All of us had plans for the week. I was wrapping up my fieldwork with only one community left to document, and I was making plans to do archival research at the University of Puerto Rico and the General Archives in San Juan. That weekend I was planning to go kayaking with my brothers and possibly do a river tour afterward with my best friend. My in-laws, Carmen and Miguel Sr., were excited about going to see the movie *Broche de Oro* at the local cinema.

Fig. 8.5. Obligatory "Mary and Joseph meeting at the manger" memes appeared on September 17 and 18.

But by the next morning, September 18, the hurricane had gained extraordinary speed and was continuing to intensify. Each three-hour bulletin only offered consternation and a deepening sense of dread and urgency. María was not going to make landfall on Thursday after all, but on Wednesday or maybe even Tuesday night. Time for preparation was very short. Most of our provisions were already stocked up, we assumed. We had plenty of batteries, camping lamps, a four-hundred-gallon cistern on the roof, and bottled water.

My in-laws live in a relatively privileged location away from flooding, landslides, and the stronger winds in the mountains. Their house is made of concrete blocks with a reinforced concrete roof. Still, we could not afford to be careless. We gave the house as thorough a cleaning as possible, neatly storing the outdoor furniture. We didn't know when we would be able to clean again, and during the storm, in the darkness of shuttered windows, the space had to be as safe as possible in case we needed to run.

I chose to stay with my in-laws this time because Miguel, an only child, was in Indiana. My brothers were helping Mom board up the house in

Aguadilla; I hoped they would be safe. I had lived through many hurricanes and tropical storms before, but I knew this was the strongest I would experience as of yet and the first I would face as an adult. It would also be the strongest hurricane to make landfall on Puerto Rico in the era of social media and cell phones, a detail that would become relevant later.

The air was hot and still in the days before the storm. By Tuesday morning, the sky was gray. We could hear hammers and drills in the distance as our neighbors dismantled their small patio roof and stored their plants indoors. Unlike my grandfather, who had relied on the historic barraca in his childhood, most people today were going to weather the hurricane in their concrete homes or evacuate to a shelter or to a relative's home.

By Tuesday evening, with provisions ready and the house as clean and secure as we could make it, we had a final meal with fresh meat and produce. We printed documents that required hard copies (including sudoku puzzles to combat boredom) and stored everything that would not be needed in the following days.

It was also time to say goodbye to friends and family before we lost connection. I called my mother, grandparents, siblings, and friends. I sent a final message on Facebook telling people not to worry about me. The house was as sealed as it could be, but I could still hear early gusts of wind outside. As I curled up in the living room and chatted with Miguel, I was suddenly plunged into darkness. I told him that I should conserve my battery but would call later. When I finally settled down in bed with Che, our Chihuahua, and tried calling Miguel to say goodbye, phone service was gone. For the next twenty-eight days, my in-laws and I would have to rely mainly on our accumulated knowledge, lore, and creativity to keep us alive.

During

I woke with a start. The room was completely dark. It took me a few seconds to get my bearings before I realized that a strong gust of wind was driving a fine mist of water into my face. The bed was just underneath a set of aluminum Miami-style windows that we had rolled shut but not boarded up. What time was it? Three in the morning? Five? Eight? The gust felt like hurricane winds, but it was too early. My first instinct was to bolt from the room, which suddenly felt unsafe. Instead, I slowly got up and turned on my small plastic battery-operated lantern. I found my field notes, computer, and hard drive and stored them in my backpack while I put most of my paper documents in a ziplock bag.

In the darkness and with the wind roaring outside, I moved my things to a small room in the middle of the house. This room, with no windows facing outside, was the safest place in the building. Carmen and Miguel Sr. were already up and about. It was roughly 6:00 a.m., and they were getting breakfast and coffee ready in the dark kitchen. Carmen had set up a makeshift cooking station, which we would use over the next few weeks, placing a small portable gas stove with two burners on the kitchen counter and two coolers filled with ice on the floor. She prepared coffee as usual. In the weeks to come, we would keep up this daily food routine as much as possible.

The entire house was boarded up except for a small acrylic window over the front door. This window, partially protected by the porch walls, provided a tiny amount of light without the danger of blowing in. The three of us settled down between the living room and dining room, placing the radio and a lantern on the dining table. I sat down with my field notebook, map, and a sudoku puzzle to pass the time. The next twenty-four hours were a combination of boredom and high adrenaline caused by constant alertness. Writing down everything that stood out to me on the radio and plotting coordinates during the weather update every three hours distracted me from thinking of my family and friends who were going through the same experience in their own isolation. Hopefully, the windows in Mom's house were holding up, my grandmother hadn't tried walking through the exposed corridors of her nursing home, my friend was up to date on his dialysis, and my brothers were safe indoors. It was a losing battle against a checklist of things I could not control.

After scolding Miguel Sr. for stepping into the marquesina to peek at the storm and get a breath of fresh air, Carmen decided she wanted to see for herself. She placed a stepladder by the door to look out through the small acrylic window. Her curiosity was understandable: we were in dark isolation, accompanied by a constant roar outside, which was punctured occasionally by the clang of something being torn away or clattering loudly down the street. After Carmen took a look, we kept the stepladder near the door, and roughly once an hour, we would peek out and I would film for about a minute on my cell phone. The ornamental palm trees in our neighbor's yard were bent at a forty-five-degree angle but would bend even farther when a *ráfaga*, a stronger gale, would blow through. It was still morning, and we were isolated even from our next-door neighbors. At 9:30 a.m., I wrote in my notebook: "The concrete walls are vibrating. It feels like an earthquake.

Fig. 8.6. During the storm, there is not much to do but wait on high alert, plot the course of the storm on a map, and write down any news heard on the radio.

The house is shaking . . . it feels like everything is going to shatter." And a little later: "Everything seems to want to fall. A monster roars. My heart is with Mom and my family. My soul is with Miguel. How can I let them know that we are well . . . how can I know if my family is well? The radio is like an anchor to humanity."

The three of us trusted and hoped our preparations were enough for the storm. It was only 10:00 a.m., and time was becoming sluggish. I wondered how the communities I was researching were holding up, worried about my interlocutors and their loved ones. Had their houses survived? Were the zinc sheets flying over us traveling miles and miles all the way from Barrio Dominguito? According to the radio, rivers were breaking flood records. There were reports of whole communities flooding, and Ada Monzón (2017) reported "está lloviendo sobre mojado" ("it is raining over wet"), referencing the oversaturation of the ground, the rising rivers, and the record-breaking floods occurring throughout the entire island.

The temperature inside the house had changed as well. Summer and early fall had been extraordinarily hot, with a humidity index of 116 degrees Fahrenheit in Arecibo during the day. The heat had been exacerbated in the

Fig. 8.7. During the worst of the storm, one can barely see outside. The wind is ripping away anything that is not tightly secured, and the roar of the wind is accompanied by tearing noises and the clanking of random objects being dragged across the street.

days before the storm as the air stilled around the house; it had worsened when we boarded up most of the windows, leaving very little air to circulate. During the storm, as the pressure went down and the wind picked up, we could feel cool rivulets of air snaking around our feet, as if María was trying to get a feel for everything inside the building. The closed aluminum windows shook, and Miguel Sr. spent much of the morning reinforcing window frames with transversally placed sticks and metal bars.

Even with advances in technology, hurricane tracking and prediction continued to be challenging. The strongest winds were supposed to strike Arecibo at around 2:00 p.m., when the hurricane's eye would begin its exit from Puerto Rico somewhere over the north coast. It was still morning when most radio stations began going off-air. Ada Monzón and the three-hour bulletins went quiet when her station, WKAQ 580, incurred heavy damage to its infrastructure. The eye was predicted to exit somewhere in a sixty-mile region between Aguadilla and Dorado: we were right in the middle of this and had very little information coming in. We would find out later that Puerto Rico's Doppler radar had been completely destroyed earlier in the day and that our friends and family outside Puerto Rico had no access to information whatsoever.

El Ojo

With less and less information trickling in and the terrifying winds growing steadily, we became more dependent on folk knowledge to provide expectations of what we would be witnessing and what we should do and avoid doing for the next few hours. Carmen, Miguel Sr., and I knew that the *ojo*, the deceptively calm eye of the storm, should be crossing over or near us in the early afternoon. It was of no surprise then that after some of the strongest gales yet, the wind suddenly became a light breeze and the torrential rain turned into a drizzle. The sky was still lead gray, but the noise and destruction had stopped. Growing up, I had heard cautionary tales, warnings against becoming overconfident when calm came after the roaring wind.

The main danger of the eye is that the seduction of calm after hours of terror would draw people outside, where they would be caught as wind speeds accelerated from zero to over one hundred miles per hour in a matter of minutes. There was no way of knowing whether the calm would last twenty minutes or two hours, whether the eye had split in two, whether we would experience the full eye or just a corner of it. Miguel Sr. and I ventured out into the marquesina so that Che could use the bathroom. Our neighbors let their dogs out into the yard.

But they called them back just as the winds began picking up again.

La Virazón

One reason the eye is considered so treasonous and dangerous is that it is followed by *la virazón*, a 180-degree switch in wind direction when the opposite side of the hurricane strikes. This is due to the circular motion of the storm. If the wind had been hitting us from south to north in the morning, it was now coming north to south at maximum velocity. Buildings, trees, and any other structures that had already been weakened by the onslaught of wind could be ripped apart at this moment. Tornadoes often form around the eye as well, so after the calm, as we were experiencing la virazón, we had to stay alert for another few hours.

While we weathered the rest of the storm, the single radio station we had left, WAPA 680, provided snippets of news throughout the island: nineteen

Fig. 8.8. The small ornamental palm trees in the neighbor's yard were bent almost ninety degrees northward during the first half of the storm; they stilled during the calm at the eye of the storm and then bent almost ninety degrees in the opposite direction with the *virazón*. These little palms were almost unscathed after almost thirty hours of wind.

police officers stranded on a roof in the town of Ciales, a family crushed in their homes by a boulder, drownings in Toa Baja, the first birth in Cabo Rojo in almost half a century (Rodríguez Fernández 2017, 22). Miguel Sr. speculated that the entirety of Arecibo's downtown was flooded because of the combined rising waters of the Arecibo River and the *marejada ciclónica*, the storm surge, that always flooded the region. The extent of the flooding, it would later be noted on the news, was record-breaking. In fact, Puerto Rico's topography would be permanently altered.

The governor issued a curfew beginning at 6:00 p.m. and lasting through the following day. At that hour, Arecibo was still getting hurricane winds, and it was hard to conceive of anyone wanting to loot in those conditions, but the strongest winds had already begun abating on the eastern side of the island. Reports of break-ins and looting were starting to crop up in the metropolitan

Fig. 8.9. "My father-in-law and Che (the Chihuahua) listening to the radio"—a sketch from the field notebook.

area. Ironically, my main reaction to that news was not concern over the potential looting but rather curiosity about how people in San Juan were able to complain when we couldn't even get a message to our next-door neighbors.

We ate dinner by the light of small plastic lanterns. Carmen preferred them to candles, which could fall over and cause a fire. It was a warm dinner, cooked on the gas stovetop, and we put the leftovers in one of the coolers. During the following days, we would learn that food must be eaten immediately unless we could give the leftovers to our neighbors.

With the sound of the waning yet still strong winds and rain lashing at the windows, there was little to do. I played sudoku a bit, marked the latest coordinates over the Atlantic Ocean, and went to bed. The house had withstood the storm. Tomorrow we would know the extent of the damage and try to contact our loved ones. For now, all I could do was rest.

After

Going Outside

The silence was the first sign that the danger was passing: no more wind and just a very light rain. It was time to open what windows we could, survey the damage, and help out our friends and neighbors. The first day after a hurricane is one of assessment and caution. Hurricanes are so large that there is often cloud coverage for days afterward, and there is always the threat of one final violent downpour or gust before the sky clears up.

The rivers were swollen and would remain so for days. The oversaturated earth was unstable, and roads were impassable, blocked by fallen trees, posts, and cables. We knew that after a storm it was normal for electricity and water to be out. In the 1980s and 1990s, we had relied on landlines to contact emergency services and family. However, this was the first hurricane to strike Puerto Rico since most people had switched over to smartphones; the unintended consequence was that communications virtually disappeared because cell phone antennas were destroyed. Even the few surviving landlines were out of service during the first week. We were completely disconnected from the outside world and had little way to gauge the scale of the damage from within our protected home.

The house was dark. All the windows were still closed and covered. Carmen prepared coffee as she had done every day before the storm—and would continue doing after. The small gas stovetop became a fixture in the kitchen. All she needed was ground coffee, water, and milk to make *café con leche*, the delectable morning drink that was a staple of the Puerto Rican diet, predating conveniences such as electricity and modern stoves. In order to prepare our most important drink of the day, she brought out *la media*, the stocking, a cloth funnel made of sturdy fabric with a metal rod, traditionally used in much of Latin America. A process that took five minutes with an electric coffee maker now took half an hour. Storing the leftover milk to prevent spoiling became another problem. All the little daily processes that we once took for granted became time-consuming projects.

Even with these changes, everything looked normal inside the house. Curiosity got the better of me. I grabbed my umbrella and camera and stepped into the front yard to survey the damage. If we were to use our specific street in Vista Azul, Arecibo, as a gauge of the disaster, everything was normal. Some zinc sheets were strewn on the ground, some plants had toppled over, and the street was slick with *hojarasca*, a mix of leaves and

Fig. 8.10. Coffee preparation with the stocking (*la media*) and a coffee maker's glass carafe.

water. But the buildings looked intact, as did the ornamental bushes and palm trees.

However, I could hear the buzzing of electric saws and people shouting, and just twenty steps over, at the next street, the scene changed completely. A fallen tree was blocking the entire street. A large group of neighbors were cutting it into pieces using electric saws and machetes. I walked one more street over, and the same scene repeated itself, and so on in every street. I quickly returned to the house and helped Carmen and Miguel Sr. clear the yard of debris and fallen plants. Zinc sheets littered the backyard; we never found out whether they came from our next-door neighbor or from two towns over.

Still early in the day, Miguel Sr. and I were itching to see if anything was open. Perhaps we could get some fresh food and gain a better idea of the devastation. We headed out to Barranca Bakery, a two-minute car drive away. This was our first real glimpse of the extent of the devastation that surrounded us. Most light posts had fallen. Small wooden second-story add-ons known as *altos* were either partially or completely destroyed. Trees had fallen over on the road, and cables were strewn everywhere. Traffic was slow because of the hazardous driving conditions, but even with the devastation,

Fig. 8.11. Many concrete homes have a second-story wood addition, and these often suffered severe damage from the storm.

we made it to the bakery relatively quickly and found a line of people outside. This was our first queue of many. The bakery was in full production, the family having weathered the storm inside their business, finding it safer than staying home. In fact, at the time they weren't even sure if they had a home to go back to, but they had diesel for the generator and stores of water and flour to make bread.

It was good to know that at least one bakery close to us was open but heartbreaking to know that it didn't ensure food access to others nearby. Later on, I remember reading a newspaper article about a woman walking hours on end to find food for her children. The local radio would report the story of another woman walking two hours each way to Arecibo's main plaza to get a warm meal for her family.

Chatting with people in line at the bakery, I gained a more comprehensive idea of how dire the financial situation was for so many on the island. Cash was now required for any sort of food or resource shopping, but because of the economic crisis, many people were already living check to check. Hurricane María landed just before payday, leaving people cash-strapped and with no source of funds, no system to access their own money, no knowledge even of whether they still had a job to return to. Informal communication with people in line became the staple for knowledge transmission and a form of communal therapeutic bonding when long-distance communication was all but nonexistent. It was a space of tension, grief, information exchange, and sometimes joy when friends or family members bumped into one another. It became a survival mechanism over the next month.

After the hurricane, we had to plan all our activities around daylight hours, approximately 6:00 a.m. until 6:00 p.m. The following is more or less the daily routine we established during this time. We got up with the sunrise, had café con leche, and drove out to a carefully chosen destination to find one resource, usually food, water, cash, or gasoline. If we had time in the afternoon, we would check up on family members. I continuously checked my phone for a signal, switching airplane mode off and on throughout the day. At around four in the afternoon, we would each take a gallon of water and bathe before the sun set. Once the landlines were reestablished about a week later, I would trek to the house of Titi Neri, Miguel's aunt, to try to call Miguel or my mother. We then had dinner in the evening and listened to the radio, played sudoku, and chatted before going to bed around 9:30 p.m. Sleeping was difficult: there was little to no breeze between 8:00 p.m. and 2:00 a.m., which made nights unbearably hot. We repeated this process daily until it felt like an unending cycle of despair.

There was a curfew on that first day, which we promptly broke by standing in the middle of the street in the darkness, chatting with all our neighbors. That night, we knew who the people around us were. There was less fear for our own safety than concern for our loved ones in the distance. Everyone was still shaken by the hurricane winds from just twenty-four hours earlier. We were on our own, millions of people seemingly stranded on a "deserted" island.

Food

During that first week after the storm, we began getting a clearer image of the extent of the devastation, along with a sense of how slow help would be to trickle in. Lack of communication was still a huge problem. I did not know whether my mother and brothers were OK; I could only assume that the house wasn't too heavily damaged. I didn't know how friends with grave health concerns were holding up or how my extended family was doing. My grandparents were in a nursing home in Ponce, on Puerto Rico's southern coast; radio commentators worried about the lack of information coming from Ponce. But they also worried about lack of communication from Arecibo, and I knew that those around me in Arecibo were more or less OK. I was almost more concerned about Miguel, who did not know that we were in good health and spirits those first days.

Regardless of how concerned we were for our loved ones, we had to continue churning away with the new routine, getting it down to a science as the days went on. We had to be careful with food and battery consumption. We couldn't save leftovers, and we only had our battery stores to rely on.

Our food stores were based on our preparations for Hurricane Irma, rather than for María, and would not hold up to the long-term scale of the emergency at hand. Having been hit hard by the storm, our local Hatillo Cash and Carry supermarket was closed, but their store one town over was open for business. Traveling there became an excursion. The main artery, State Road 2, had no streetlights; most were wrecked and on the ground, and buildings were completely flattened. The theater, where my in-laws had been planning to watch a movie just sixty hours earlier, was missing two walls; we could see the ocean right through it. Gas stations looked like crumpled paper, their metal structures completely destroyed. Cables were strewn all over the road, and electricity posts that hadn't completely fallen were dangling precariously over fearful drivers. People drove extra slowly and carefully, aware that if there was an accident, there would be no way to call for help and no assurance that hospitals would be operational.

The supermarket itself was well stocked and brightly lit, getting its power from a diesel-operated generator. There were crowds of people replenishing their provisions, enjoying respite from the heat, some finding one another for the first time since the storm, sobbing, telling each other stories of loss and destruction. People sitting outside had brought multi-plug extension cords and were charging their phones. The space was crowded, but even with the hustle and bustle, conversations felt muted compared to other days. I saw a good friend and was relieved to hear that her family was well. This was the only time we went to the supermarket in the first month without having to stand in line. The rules had yet to be set, the pre-storm food stock was still plentiful, and we had cash and gasoline.

Not long after returning to the house, I began writing Miguel a letter to let him know we were doing well; I hoped I could mail it in the next few days. Just as I was finishing up, I heard someone outside call my name. I had no idea who it could be—most of my friends were far away. A young woman I had never seen before jumped out of the back of a van and asked if I was Gloria, Miguel's wife. She quickly told me she was one of Miguel's childhood friends; she had come down from San Juan to check up on her father and was taking the opportunity to check up on us as well. She couldn't stay long but took my letter and also took a picture of all of us. As the van started to pull away, all of our neighbors came running out clutching small notes with their names and the phone numbers of family members to contact. It was our first contact with the outside world, and we were left feeling both relieved and extremely emotional. I would get to see the photo on Facebook about a month later—and seeing it in the digital context would be as emotional as the moment it was taken.

Water

Clean drinking water is a precious resource that, until recently, has been taken for granted in much of the United States and to a certain extent in Puerto Rico. Many people, including my in-laws, had cisterns on the roofs of their houses, not just for hurricane season but as a safeguard for increasingly unreliable water supplies; extensive droughts during the last few years had led to strict water rationing in large parts of the island. We were lucky that our cistern had survived the raging winds unscathed. Others were not so lucky.

Most of Puerto Rico's landscape, especially in the northern and eastern regions, is lush and rainy. Fresh water was traditionally accessed from rivers, streams, wells, and natural springs or collected in stone and concrete cisterns called *aljibes*. A series of manufactured lakes built during the twentieth century provide most of the water to the population. Many of the pumps that moved water throughout the island either relied on the collapsed electrical system or had suffered extensive damage during the storm.

The night before the hurricane rolled in, I had talked to a good friend who lives in Japan. He wanted to check up on me and my family and told me that at least he was relatively calm about his own family in the mountain town of Utuado. They had "secured the horses and checked the natural springs." It sounded a bit melodramatic at the time, but these land-based preparations proved to be essential for survival. Many places in Utuado were cut off because of landslides, collapsed bridges, and flooding.

Residents of Arecibo's urban and suburban barrios didn't have the advantage of pure spring water or even rain during the first week or so. Hurricane María was so large it sucked away all the air and moisture over an incredible expanse, changing weather patterns for roughly a week. We had cisterns, but there were rumors that our area of Arecibo would not get water service until October or even November. Three days after the storm, a radio station transmitting from San Juan announced distribution centers throughout Puerto Rico, including Arecibo. Miguel Sr. and I headed out to the indicated location and instead found blocked roads and helpful but very confused police officers. Dejected, we returned home having wasted a bit more precious gasoline on a fruitless mission.

Our next-door neighbor later told us that she had heard there was water available at two official places, the first about ten miles away in Barrio Hato Viejo, where the main water company plant was located, and the second about three miles away at Sector Rodríguez Olmos, where most of the city's sporting arenas were located. According to her report, there was a church allowing people to fill up their water receptacles and maybe a government-sanctioned pump in the area. Rodríguez Olmos, it turned out, was one of the very few places in Arecibo that never lost running water. Ironically and tragically, it was also completely devastated by the flooding of the Río Grande de Arecibo; many people who lived in the area lost most if not all of their belongings. We eventually found a large water pump with trucks lined up behind it. One of the trucks was being filled up, and they were allowing people with small canisters and jugs to get water from a spigot on the back. The line was short, but people were anxious. This was a new experience for everyone. We were eventually able to fill up our milk gallons and other jugs and were told that they would be back the next day.

When we returned a few days later, there was a different man standing near the pump, and he explained kindly that this pump was only for large cistern trucks and not for individuals. He had no idea who had told us otherwise, and he suggested we go elsewhere. A local man walked up and chimed in that if we wanted water, all we had to do was go to the men's bathroom at the basketball stadium just a block away, and so after giving each other apprehensive looks, we did.

We parked the car on the caked river mud at the stadium parking lot. There was indeed a line to the men's bathroom consisting of *arecibeños* from all walks of life carrying bottles, gallons, and even plastic cat litter jugs to fill with water. Some people even had shopping carts. In a show of solidarity, an off-duty police officer from the neighborhood had brought his own garden hose to connect to one of the pipes in the men's bathroom and was coordinating the inflow of people. The building itself was heavily damaged from the storm. The interior had a crust of dried mud that was becoming mucky from the water slopping over the receptacles being carried back and forth. The roof was partially gone, and we had to tread carefully to avoid cutting ourselves with debris. I volunteered to enter the men's bathroom to minimize the number of people in what had become a noisy, muddy cavern. The four sinks had their in-lines disconnected and were freely pouring water onto the floor or into whatever receptacles were put under them. The jugs filled quickly but would get messy if they touched the ground. People were quiet, helping one another and trying to avoid confrontation, even with the sweltering heat and bees buzzing around us. People who knew one another chatted; those who didn't also chatted until they did. We carried eight or ten gallons of water to the car to be used for washing laundry, flushing the toilets, and bathing. We also helped another person who had a lot of water to carry. We arrived home exhausted, muddy, and sweaty, knowing we would have to repeat the process in a few days. Repeat it we would, but never in the same place.

A few days later, we heard from another neighbor that there would be water distribution in the town plaza. Miguel Sr., Carmen, and I arrived early with our plastic milk gallons and a five-gallon paint tub. Eight days had passed since María had landed, and it was the first time we observed the city government present and actively supplying food and water. After some initial chaos, we waited in the prescribed line (there were separate lines for cooked food, Federal Emergency Management Agency [FEMA] food packs, and potable water). Again, people were relatively calm, although slightly more impatient than before. The water truck arrived a few hours later than announced, and it took a while before a distribution system was devised for both large and small water receptacles. It was hard to know who was in charge, but even as the threat of quarrels brewed, people generally helped one another and made sure that everybody left with their containers filled. We did not get in line for warm food or FEMA food packs because we felt that other people needed them much more than we did. The hot food, mainly rice with picnic sausages, turned out to be the only hot meal many people had eaten in days. Not everyone could afford to have an electric generator or even a small gas stove like ours.

The FEMA packs consisted mostly of expired canned foods, but people took them gratefully, as it was the only food available for many. Supermarkets

Fig. 8.12. It became an almost daily routine to wait patiently in line for provisions, often for anywhere between three and ten hours.

were slowly opening, often with long queues and limited supplies; without electricity and with what felt like 100-degree-Fahrenheit heat, storing perishables was not an option. Furthermore, supermarkets required cash, which was in low supply even for people who were still going to work or had savings. Most banks had been heavily damaged, and even the ones that had working generators didn't have internet or a steady supply of cash. A bank line could last anywhere from two to sixteen hours. We joked that we were becoming so used to queuing that we would miss the experience when normalcy was reestablished.

Arecibo's ice factory, located in the historic city center, eventually reopened. We drove by early in the morning, saw the longest line we had seen in our lives—possibly over one thousand people—and returned home. We would continue drinking our water warm and eating canned foods for as long as necessary.

It didn't rain that first week, but eventually we began getting our usual afternoon thunderstorms. This meant we didn't have to guess where water might be distributed every other day. We cut the drainage pipes and placed buckets underneath each one around the house when the sky began getting cloudy. They would fill up quickly once it started raining, and we would pour the water into the plastic gallon jugs to avoid mosquito infestations. All of our neighbors had variations of this system using any available container, from large trash bins to paddling pools. It was not ideal drinking water, but it was water nonetheless.

Bathing and Laundry

Water is precious not only for drinking but also for maintaining one's own hygiene and cleanliness of space. This became a critical priority at a time when we were hearing reports of deaths from leptospirosis and the ever-present threat of contagion. Water had to be used judiciously even when we were able to fill our gallons at a designated oasis or when rain was bountiful. We used only the cleanest water for drinking and cooking. The rest we used for bathing and laundry. And then we recycled leftover laundry water for mopping.

Before the mid-twentieth century when electricity and washing machines became accessible to most households, women traditionally washed clothing by hand, often at the river's edge. Because of high electric bills, many people continued air-drying, using the tropical sun and trade winds to leave clothes feeling warm and toasty. While waiting in one of the many interminable queues, I met women who told me they were going to the river to wash, but neither Carmen nor I dared take the risk of leptospirosis; instead, we relied on two five-gallon paint tubs to wash laundry. We used one to wash and another to rinse, and then we would wring the clothes between the two of us, or sometimes three if Miguel Sr. was around. Carmen had always air-dried her clothes and had perfected the system. We could see our neighbors doing the same, washing in their backyard and filling the clotheslines on sunny mornings.

The lack of water and electricity brought about the creative reintroduction of washing traditions. There were news reports of families making and selling PVC washboards to sustain themselves. Waiting in line, people would share washing techniques, such as using a five-gallon paint bucket as we were doing, along with a clean plunger dedicated exclusively to laundry purposes. One woman said that clothing came out cleaner than with a washing machine and that it was slightly less work than washing by

Fig. 8.13. Five-gallon paint tubs and designated plungers became a faster way of cleaning favored by many people and spread through verbal communication. Various families began making wood and PVC washboards to sell for some income.

hand. Titi Neri recommended that we heat our bathing-water jugs by placing them in the afternoon sun for two hours. This informal system of sharing advice, knowledge, and information through casual encounters became vital to making life a little easier.

Communication

Communication was slowly being reestablished. By the end of the second week, there were multiple radio stations, including a local one. These stations provided information about what was happening in the greater world, but it was a one-sided type of communication. When people wanted to talk to us or we wanted to talk to them, they had to come to us, or we had to go to them.

I kept my cell phone on airplane mode and would check for a signal every few hours. A few days after the storm, I got a bit of signal on my phone. I dialed and dialed until I got Miguel . . . or was it Miguel? There was someone on the other line sobbing and asking, "Mami? Mami?" I called again and heard someone ask where to get ice. Then the signal was gone. When I could get any signal at all, the lines would often be scrambled and distorted with haunting voices echoing the same anxieties I felt.

I was not able to talk to my mother until over a week after the storm, when her landline began functioning again; even then, I had to walk to Titi Neri's house and use the only working landline in the house. It wasn't until a few weeks in that we began getting spotty cell phone service, and still the lines would often be crossed, and I would have to dial up to thirty times before getting a tone. Neighbors and friends would indicate a particular spot on the highway or by the hospital or a store where there was a signal. These spots did not always prove functional, but the rumors spread, and there would often be ten or twenty cars parked on either side of the road near these "miraculous" spots.

I still remember crying the first time Miguel and I were able to talk on the phone. He was in the car with our friend Jeff in Indiana, and I heard him say, "Glori? Glori?" before we both burst into tears. It took days and often weeks before I was able to contact other family members, and it would be forty days before I was able to talk to my grandparents. There is little to prepare you for the profound feeling of relief when you hear a loved one's voice after weeks of tragedy. It is a feeling that ironically can be as acute and painful as the tragedy itself.

Pain and Humor: Animals, Helicopters, Deaths, and Jokes

Every aspect of life was affected, down to the smallest details. The loudest sounds every day were the helicopters flying over our neighborhood, headed to destinations unknown. They flew right over us multiple times a day but never stopped anywhere near Arecibo's urban areas. I later learned that many of these helicopters were either moving between San Juan and Aguadilla or taking supplies to inaccessible communities in the island's interior. The helicopters were the only sign of external help during the first few weeks, but they never stopped near us.

The local fauna was affected by the storm. When trees fell and leaves were ripped away, birds, bees, and iguanas struggled to find shelter, often heading for neighborhoods and houses. We quickly learned that bees were attracted to coffee, even without sugar. Sure signs that an iguana, often measuring up to four feet in length, had entered someone's yard or porch

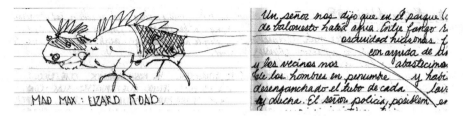

Fig. 8.14. "Mad Max: Lizard Road"—a sketch from the field notebook.

were the piercing sounds of yells and laughter. These large invasive reptiles are not aggressive but have a mean tail whiplash. Whenever they appeared in or near our yard, Carmen would call her neighbors to shoo them away with brooms. Everyone would come out, and it would become an occasion for gossip, laughter, and consternation.

Humor, especially improvised humor made up of witty commentary and sarcastic responses, was critical to diffusing tense situations and making the intolerable livable. Finding our drabbest clothing to clean the roof could easily become a fashion show. Making people in line giggle at some silly observation became an icebreaker. Even gallows humor provided relief from almost daily news of the deaths of loved ones, neighbors, or acquaintances.

With so much tragic news combined with a lack of adequate communication, feelings of impotence and psychological pain only grew. We would find out, usually days after the fact, that an older family member had passed away, or that people in the region were dying from lack of dialysis. There was no way to commemorate the deceased because funeral homes were inaccessible. People were quickly and quietly buried or cremated.

Epilogue (Leaving)

My in-laws and I left Puerto Rico twenty-eight days after Hurricane María made landfall. Leaving was hard for many reasons. I had not been able to complete my dissertation research: there were communities I did not document, archives left unexplored, interlocuters I could not meet. My mother-in-law was anxious to return to her normal routine, but there was uncertainty about when or whether her work would resume. The only way to convince my parents-in-law to leave was to set a return date for one month later. We lived in one of the first communities to get electricity back, but there was still no water or even the assurance of getting water in the following weeks. My husband and I wanted his parents to recuperate after the compounded traumatic events of the storm and the postapocalyptic living conditions we had struggled through. The stress of standing in line for hours under the sweltering sun and carrying gallons of water every day was enough to precipitate a heart attack or a stroke, either of which could prove lethal with the precarious health care system. The constant news of death and suffering made the need to leave all the more pressing.

More than thirty phone calls, multiple battery charges, and many resounding headaches later, we were able to get flights off the island for three humans and Che. Ever one to be fully prepared, Carmen made sure the house was watched over, medicines prepared for the next months, and transportation secured to the airport. The still-spotty communication services made these simple tasks exponentially more complicated. Miguel would meet us in Newark, New Jersey, where we would stay with his extended family. The Newark-based family had, like much of the Puerto Rican diaspora, been sending huge care packages to the island since the storm and were coordinating as much help as they could from what felt like an impossible distance.

Traveling to San Juan gave us a glimpse of how the hurricane had completely changed the landscape. San Juan itself looked almost normal compared to the rest of the island . . . almost. Military vehicles, trucks with FEMA provisions, and convoys were a common sight. The Luis Muñoz Marín Airport felt as if it were located in another time and place, simultaneously the airport I had known all of my life and yet completely different. There was electricity, air-conditioning, and water. The floors and ceilings seemed to gleam, even with evident storm damage. It almost felt like a slice of normalcy—until I paid attention to the people coming in and out. Half of them looked like military from the United States and other countries, ripped straight out of an action movie or war-zone news clip. The other half were Puerto Rican families and their pets leaving the island amid tears and uncertain futures. There were more elderly people than I had ever seen at the airport, more wheelchairs than I had ever known were possible. At our gate, the airline employees were struggling to find enough people who spoke English to sit in the exit rows on our flight. Many families and elderly people who had never planned to leave Puerto Rico suddenly found themselves leaving with no idea of when or if they would ever be able to return.

Fig. 8.15. Elderly people wait calmly in long lines of wheelchairs by the flight gates. This scene was repeated for each flight leaving Puerto Rico.

The flight itself was uneventful. Our family reunion was sweet and emotional.

Since then, we have been processing the devastation we witnessed, rebuilding when possible, and helping loved ones as well as strangers. I don't have nightmares about the storm, but in my waking hours, I see repeating loops of the buildings around me being destroyed by imaginary winds. The struggle isn't over yet. There is much rebuilding to be done, mourning for those we lost, and every hurricane season there is the terror of another storm. Puerto Ricans will continue to use their accumulated lore and their stories and their experiences, filling in the repertoire of necessary knowledge to survive the next event.

Notes

*All artwork by the author.

1. Translated from Spanish; all translations by the author.

References

Behar, Ruth. 1996. *The Vulnerable Observer: Anthropology That Breaks Your Heart.* Boston: Beacon.

Boose, Emery R., Mayra I. Serrano, and David R. Foster. 2004. "Landscape and Regional Impacts of Hurricanes in Puerto Rico." *Ecological Monographs* 74 (2): 335–52.

Monzón, Ada. 2017. *Noticias.* Broadcast on WKAQ-580 AM San Juan, September 20, 2017.

Rodríguez Fernández, Perla. 2017. "Edición del 22 de septiembre de 2017." *El Vocero*, September 22, 2017. https://issuu.com/vocero.com/docs/v0922001.

Science Reference Section, Library of Congress. 2019. "Is the Old Adage 'Red Sky at Night, Sailor's Delight. Red Sky in Morning, Sailor's Warning' True, or Is It Just an Old Wives' Tale?" Library of Congress, November 19, 2019. https://www.loc.gov/item/is-the-old-adage-red-sky-at-night-sailors-delight-red-sky-in-morning-sailors-warning-true-or-is-it-just-an-old-wives-tale/.

Gloria M. COLOM BRAÑA studied architecture and historic preservation. She is a doctoral candidate at Indiana University currently researching creative uses of traditional architecture through folkloristics.

CONCLUSION

The COVID-19 Pandemic and
"Folklife's First Responders"

Georgia Ellie Dassler, with Kate Parker Horigan

A s Carl Lindahl articulates in chapter 1, contributors to this
volume address questions about how survivors and ethnographers respond to disaster. During the course of revisiting these essays as editors,
we have also been living through the global COVID-19 pandemic, which
provides another lens through which to view the roles of survivors and ethnographers in situations of crisis. Given the geographic reach and the dura-
tion of the pandemic, we are now faced even more with the notion that "we
are all survivors." In that light, we returned in particular to Lindahl's third
series of questions from chapter 1: "What is the role of the ethnographer in
a disaster-stricken community? Is it to describe, document, advocate, or
respond? What can we do as professionals? What should we do, and what
should we not do?"

This concluding chapter explores these questions by presenting the
work of Georgia Ellie Dassler, who as a master's student in folk studies
at Western Kentucky University (WKU) completed a capstone project,
"Folklife's First Responders," under the direction of Brent Björkman, director of the Kentucky Folklife Program and the Kentucky Museum at WKU.
Dassler conducted a series of interviews with public folklorists in 2020–21
to learn how they have adapted their work in the context of the COVID-19
pandemic. Their answers, synthesized below, illustrate pressing questions
and promising strategies to make future work relevant, equitable, and sus-
tainable even in overlapping contexts of ongoing crisis. In the pages that
follow, Dassler offers a summative overview of the results of her project,
which are also available in greater detail on her public website.[1]

"Folklife's First Responders"

As fieldwork was put on pause and performances and festivals were postponed or canceled, many public folklore and arts organizations and individual folklorists initiated new projects and programs, often to document or provide an outlet for collective expressions responding to the pandemic.[2] Examples include the Vermont Folklife Center's *Listening in Place*, the Center for Food and Culture's *Comfort Foodways* digital exhibit, Appalshop's *Creating in Place*, and *Naming the Lost*.[3] These projects position folklorists as first responders of their own sort.

The contributions to the present volume led me also to ask how being both survivors and responders affects folklorists and our work in the pandemic. Although this question emerged mostly in hindsight, some raised the issue in my interviews. "The tendency of folklorists is to be like 'Yes! Let's collect this!'" says Ohio State PhD candidate Sydney Varajon (2020), "and I found myself being frustrated by that. . . . We're all living in a pandemic, and why do we have to make everything *work*?" Varajon references a common sentiment among folklorists I spoke with: notwithstanding personal and professional challenges, they are confident they have a role to play in resilience and recovery efforts. In fact, they feel an "ethical and moral obligation" to play a role, even if it requires thinking and acting in new ways and even if that role is not always obvious to those outside the field (Lora Bottinelli, personal communication, February 2, 2021). As Naomi Sturm-Wijesinghe, director of the Philadelphia Folklore Project, explains, there was a "societal attitude that arts or folk arts were not vital, or that we were the icing on the cake," compared to immediate needs such as personal protective equipment, job security, rent, and food (Sturm-Wijesinghe and Morales 2020). Although Sturm-Wijesinghe acknowledges that those needs were more deserving of immediate focus, "there are various aspects to having a healthy community" (2020). National Council for Traditional Arts director Lora Bottinelli (2020) explains, "We know that participating in community-based arts and culture makes people healthier, it contributes to wellbeing."

There is a place in this pandemic-stricken reality for the kind of work that public and academic folklorists alike are accustomed to doing, such as fieldwork, arts programming and presenting, and arts grant making. For example, "just doing interviews, making people feel they have a voice, and that their concerns and stories are valid, and worth recording," can have a significant impact (Sizemore 2020). But the skills of folklorists can play an expanded role as well, as Sturm-Wijesinghe explains:

> The challenge has always been to show how folk culture is *not* the same as just arts presenting. It's not the same as just having a creative outlet, which are all great things, but this is the air we breathe, right? It's literally the work of who we are. . . . Yes, this might not be the time for a massive Gamelan and Balinese dance concert. However, access to key ingredients for nutrition, and healing, access to health care that honors traditional views, and expectations, knowing how to work with people to serve communities versus, you know, diving in and just being the savior. These are methodologies that are integral to folklore. (Sturm-Wijesinghe and Morales 2020)

The Philadelphia Folklore Project, as Sturm-Wijesinghe alludes to above, has reallocated time and resources toward working with social service organizations, making direct monetary donations when appropriate, and providing more material and technical support. "We began doing more short-range programs that weren't just about us producing stuff," she explains. "We became much more rapid-response" (Sturm-Wijesinghe and Morales 2020).

Even during the pandemic, folklorists are still producing public programs, but most have moved online. Some of these are reaching greater audiences, but in a virtual space there are also different needs to consider. As Lilli Tichinin (2020), program coordinator for Folk Arts, Arts Projects, and Accessibility at New Mexico Arts, points out, "That's one of the amazing things that going virtual has done, is really expanded the geographic range, and maybe even perhaps the age range of the audience, for some programming. But, at the same time . . . it also shrinks the audience in terms of it limits access [for] folks who don't have reliable internet. . . . There's such a wide range of capacity and technological ability." Folklorists are acutely aware of this "digital divide"—independent folklorist Judy Sizemore (2020) notes that, when partnering with organizations that provide pandemic-response resources in rural Kentucky, "the really difficult thing is that the people who we really need to be connecting with, the people who really need these services, are very difficult to reach."

Folklorists must also consider the emotional and psychological needs of would-be participants in long-distance programming. "People's bandwidth is just so decreased, right now, we have to know when not to push," says independent folklorist Thomas Grant Richardson (2020).

Varajon (2020), who started the *Pandemic Postcard Project* in the early months of lockdown, echoes these concerns: "As someone who lives somewhere where the internet is not great, or reliable, that has its own set of challenges . . . and so I wrestled with that for a bit, you know, like everybody's in these extra challenging times, and it's already hard to ask people to give you [their] time. . . . I wanted to be careful of that. Yeah, people might have been stuck at home, but they have all these different challenges and responsibilities. . . . You want it to be useful to the people who participate." Varajon designed her printable postcard template, to be decorated however participants wish, so that it is "low-tech, like it's not going to take a lot of literal bandwidth, or that much emotional bandwidth." In addition to her own academic interest in documenting how those in quarantine experience space and place, Varajon centered the *Pandemic Postcard Project* on "connectivity," attempting to address the needs of participants in isolation to express themselves creatively and connect with others.

Established public folklore organizations have taken similar approaches. One example is CityLore's *The Corona Chronicles* initiative (originally titled *Touching Hearts, Not Hands*), which solicits submissions of expressive reactions to the pandemic and other timely events, including poetry, memorials, signs protesting anti-Black police brutality, and memes.[4] One of the project's facilitators, Jake Rosenberg (2020), notes how *The Corona Chronicles*—with its nationwide, crowdsourced approach—differs from CityLore's typical projects, which are usually more localized, working in person with communities in New York City. Still, the fundamental priority of the project—paying close attention to the needs of participants and responding to them—has stayed consistent: "At the end of the day . . . it comes down to, what does the audience want?" (Rosenberg 2020). Among public projects undertaken by folklorists, those wants and needs include opportunities to be creative, chances to share personal experiences with others, and outlets for grief.

Folklorists are relying increasingly on virtual channels for intra-field communication as well, as they try to develop best practices for pivoting their work (Zoe Van Buren, personal communication, January 28, 2021). Notable among these channels is the Living Traditions Network (LTN). "A collaborative effort of traditional artists, organizations, and communities that sustain living traditions,"[5] LTN launched a website in 2020 that serves as a "Grand Central Station" for compiling artist relief and recovery resources, arts events, advocacy opportunities, and other resources (Lora

Bottinelli, personal communication, February 2, 2021). Folklorists and arts/cultural workers involved with LTN also meet monthly via Zoom to share concerns, successes, and opportunities to collaborate.

Just as the events of 2020 have called increased attention to racial, economic, and other social inequities in the nation at large, they have also done so within folklore as a discipline. Sturm-Wijesinghe describes the systemic racism and classism in American communities as "multiple pandemics" (Sturm-Wijesinghe and Morales 2020). "If there's anything good coming out of this," says Judy Sizemore (2020), "it's made us confront a lot of the problems that we have ignored" and given folklorists renewed incentive to direct their efforts toward those problems. Racial and ethnic representation within arts institutions has been a frequent topic at LTN meetings, as have the inaccessibility of grant opportunities for artists and small organizations led by people of color and other equity considerations. An early 2021 meeting, for example, addressed the fact that when it is safe to resume large in-person festivals and performances, engaging a local police presence for security may make Black and other community members of color feel *less* safe.

In a similar vein, increased reliance on virtual media has called attention to accessibility needs, such as providing captions and alternative text for online content: "There's actually a lot of things that accessibility communities, disability communities, have been asking for for a long time that are finally happening, because we're [all working] in a digital world. But there's also a lot of . . . realization that a lot of folks haven't ever thought about virtual accessibility" (Tichinin 2020). Tichinin encourages folklore and arts organizations to consider how community members who may not be able to attend an event in person because of physical access needs can participate from their own homes—to expand who they think of as being part of their constituency. Tichinin says, "I do think that this is an opportunity to sort of frame this as, this helps *everyone* gain better access."

Many interviewees pointed out how shifts in methodology and the use of technology are not an anomaly in the history of the field. "We could have had the exact same conversation in 1920," Rosenberg (2020) notes. "All of a sudden, there's film or phonograph equipment. . . . It alters the process." Thomas Grant Richardson (2020) observes, "This is just the latest shift in how we do fieldwork . . . this shift may have just happened more abruptly."[6] But folklorists' instincts to document and to engage with expressive culture, and their commitment to doing so ethically, remain consistent.

"You're using tools that already exist in your toolbox, and you're going to find new ways to make them work," says the Philadelphia Folklore Project's Eric César Morales (Sturm-Wijesinghe and Morales 2020).

At the March 2021 meeting of the LTN, discussion turned toward transitioning *back* to the formats and methods folklorists relied on before the pandemic, as more Americans received vaccines and large in-person gatherings began to seem safer. Such discussions bring relief, with folklorists admitting their reluctance to ever produce another virtual festival or attend another conference from their home offices. Still, some changes are going to be permanent, and many folklorists also welcome those changes. "Even someday when we are allowed to be in person again, it's still probably going to look different," says Tichinin (2020). "Let's not just see this as a stopgap but really see, what are the pieces of value that we can add?" From Tichinin's call for greater attention to universal accessibility to Richardson's predictions about the future of fieldwork and to virtual meetings attended by professionals on a monthly basis, there will be plenty of opportunities to continue finding those "pieces of value."

Notes

1. https://folkresponders.wordpress.com/.
2. *Folklorist* here is used as shorthand, but not everybody I interviewed has a degree in folklore or even primarily identifies as a "folklorist."
3. *Listening in Place*, https://www.vermontfolklifecenter.org/listening; *Comfort Foodways*, https://comfortfoodwaysexhibit.wordpress.com; *Creating in Place*, https://www.appalshoparchive.org/Gallery/85; *Naming the Lost*, https://namingthelost.com.
4. https://citylore.org/urban-folk-culture/the-corona-chronicles/.
5. https://www.livingtraditionsnetwork.org.
6. For webinars on virtual fieldwork techniques led by Richardson in April 2020, see https://www.facebook.com/groups/1511202559129064/permalink/2489230831326227/.

References

Bottinelli, Lora. 2020. Interview by Josephine Reed, December 10, 2020, *Art Works* podcast. https://www.arts.gov/stories/podcast/lora-bottinelli.
Richardson, Thomas Grant. 2020. Interview by Ellie Dassler, September 17, 2020, Zoom.
Rosenberg, Jake. 2020. Interview by Ellie Dassler, September 8, 2020, Zoom.
Sizemore, Judy. 2020. Interview by Ellie Dassler, October 29, 2020, Zoom.

Sturm-Wijesinghe, Naomi, and Eric César Morales. 2020. Interview by Ellie Dassler, October 28, 2020, Zoom.

Tichinin, Lilli. 2020. Interview by Ellie Dassler, September 17, 2020, Zoom.

Varajon, Sydney. 2020. Interview by Ellie Dassler, September 8, 2020, Zoom.

Georgia Ellie DASSLER is the Assistant Director for Traditional Arts at South Arts in Atlanta, Georgia. She completed her MA in Folk Studies at Western Kentucky University in 2021.

INDEX